Lisa Gill

Caput Nili

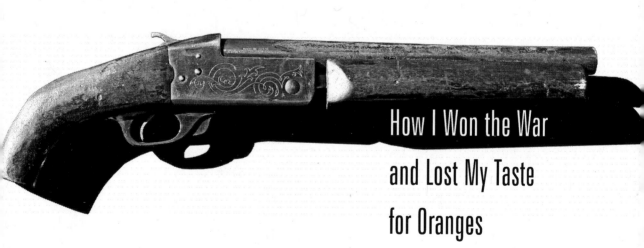

How I Won the War
and Lost My Taste
for Oranges

with art by Kris Mills

CAPUT NILI: HOW I WON THE WAR AND LOST MY TASTE FOR ORANGES

WRITTEN by Lisa Gill
ILLUSTRATED by Kris Mills

THIS BOOK was originally generated, edited, and designed by Melody Sumner Carnahan and Michael Sumner of Burning Books, working in collaboration with the artists. Copyediting was by Diane Armitage, Aline Chipman Brandauer, and Molly Beer. A limited-edition prototype released by Burning Books in 2010 (www.burningbooks.org) earned two awards for design from the New Mexico Book Association.

COVER ART BY KRIS MILLS: (front) "Woman Pouring Shotgun" after Jean-Auguste Dominique Ingres, *The Source*, 1856; (back) "Christina's Antipsychotic Linoleum" after Andrew Wyeth, *Christina's World*, 1948.

ORIGINAL BUSTS of Sigmund Freud and John Hanning Speke by Liz Hunt; busts of Martin H. Teicher and Margaret Sanger by Kris Mills.

MRI SCANS are of Lisa Gill's brain, taken in 2003.

QUOTES PAGE 6: Jaime Sabines from *Recuento de Poemas* (translated by Mitch Rayes); James Baldwin from *Notes of a Native Son*; Linda Seidel from *Jan van Eyck's Arnolfini Portrait: Stories of an Icon*.

"Say So" was originally published in *Blue Mesa Review*, Issue 21, 2008.

A RECORDING of the poetry from *Caput Nili* with music composed by Mitch Rayes is available from Reckless Faith Records at www.mitchrayes.com.

FIRST TRADE EDITION: West End Press, May 2011
ISBN: 978-0-9826968-5-9
CAPUT NILI © 2006, 2009, 2011 Lisa Gill
ARTWORK © 2009 Kris Mills

FOR BOOK INFORMATION:
West End Press, P.O. Box 27334, Albuquerque, NM 87125
www.westendpress.org

DISTRIBUTED BY:
University of New Mexico Press, Order Department 1-800-249-7737

I wish you a past you can live with.
JAIME SABINES

People are trapped in history, and history is trapped in them.
JAMES BALDWIN

...each of us is responsible for the orchestration of our own responses...
LINDA SEIDEL

Caput Nili

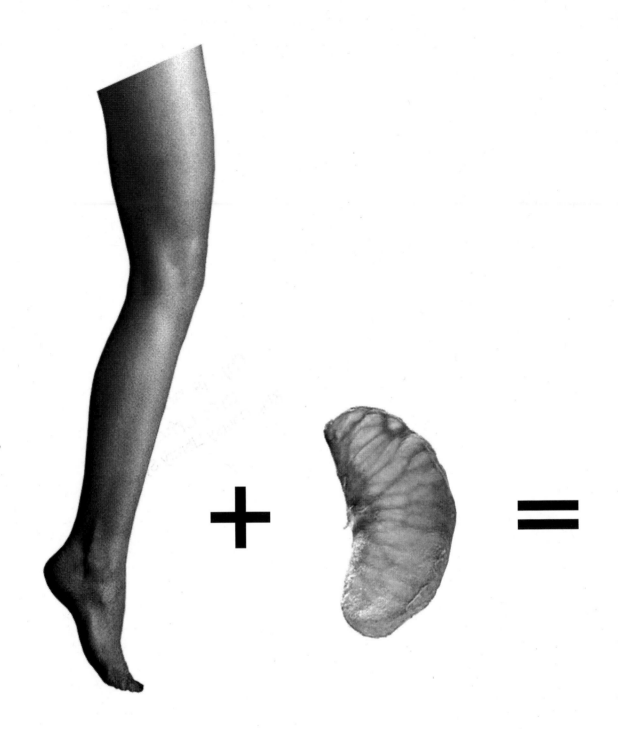

W E S T   E N D   P R E S S   2 0 1 1

FOR CENTURIES the Latin phrase *caput Nili quaerere* (literally to search for the head of the Nile) symbolized an impossible journey. After John Hanning Speke "discovered" the source of the Nile in 1858, the words *caput Nili* came to symbolize any discovery of significance. Freud used the phrase in 1896 in *The Aetiology of Hysteria* when he posited that at the root of every "case" of hysteria there were "one or more premature sexual experiences." He called the discovery of the association of trauma with mental disturbance "*a caput Nili* in neuropathology." Then he recanted. —L.G.

This book is dedicated to Virginia Hampton,
director of my one-woman *Caput Nili* show.

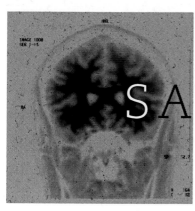

SAY SO

I always wanted to be a writer, but the first time I saw my name in print and knew it really meant something was on a pill bottle in 1989. Tofranil. That particular drug did nothing for me, but it was the beginning of a legacy. I was nineteen and I was hooked. My ears were full of psychiatrists' promises, and I believed a pill would fix me.

Since then, I have taken more head drugs than lovers.

And each time, in the beginning, there is such hope. *This is the one.* Oh Quetiapine. Oh Stelazine, Mellaril, Prozac. Oh Zoloft, Neurontin, Depakote, Ambien, and Valium. Oh Olanzapine, Clonazepam, Wellbutrin, Abilify, Remeron.

Oh and oh and oh.

Baby.

For the most part, I remember their names and side effects. Some, like Tegretol and Dilantin, I'd like to forget. Others are simply lost into the less-than-memorable category of something else that didn't work to curb my pendulous moodswings and unfettered insomnia.

*

But I always wanted to be a writer.

By fourth grade I was carrying a notebook everywhere and writing my class book reports in ballad form. By fifth grade I was devastated that no one would accept my poems for publication. By sixth grade I was the epitome of a vain poet declaring, in my journal, *I will get published yet.* I even signed and dated that entry: November 16, 1982. By eighteen the doctors had labeled me as having *hypergraphia.*

So according to them, my desire to write was just another medical condition, some electrical compulsion, some biological glitch akin to having blocked tear ducts or strep throat. For a while, I believed that *hypergraphia* explained the short stories and poems, the epic and usually unsent letters, my Xeroxed books, and the school literary journals I edited. A medical excuse seemed more legitimate than accommodating ferocious desire.

*

There is this test that psychologists administer where they show you a picture and have you tell a story with a beginning, a middle, and an end. The first time I was locked up, at twenty, I had to try to pass that test.

At the time I was a story writer, a committed proponent of the plotless wonder. I believed aesthetically in internal drama and had just learned the term *in medias res*. So when the doc showed me a picture of a boy with a violin, I said, "He's thinking about his father."

And that was it.

The doctor began to argue with me, asking for a beginning, a middle, and an end.

I argued back, first with literary aesthetics of what makes a story, and then I told him that the external environment was irrelevant, that every landscape and posture was simply host to some thought the brain was thinking.

All told, post ink blots, MMPI, EEGs, and more, the psychologist said, "You test schizophrenic but . . ." and then he kept talking, going on about how I should be diagnosed, but all I heard was, "You test *schizophrenic*."

Later I'd think literature had made me fail.

*

Before I was labeled *hypergraphic*, I was called *manic depressive*. Actually, the first time I got labeled, it was pretty gentle. I got called "*a little bit* manic depressive" by a church counselor. Looking back, what comes to mind is that old expression about horseshoes and hand grenades which I can never quite remember.

The very term *manic depressive* dates me. Now the phrasing is *bipolar*. I've grown up inside the evolution of modern psychiatry and been prey to a wide variety of fads and linguistic whims. The *bipolar* thing, though, had some resonance.

I remember when it first hit me, in eighth grade, almost a year before I saw any variety of counselor or shrink. I was eating lunch with my mother and brother. They're from the "normal" side of the family and at that time paid me little heed. Left to my own devices and bored, I dropped a grape into my glass of 7-Up.

A minute later I noticed the grape had risen to the surface of the glass, buoyed by little bubbles. As I stared at it, the grape began rolling over, releasing the carbonation to the air. When the bubbles were all gone, it fell. Once at the bottom, the cycle started over.

I recognized the pattern instantly. Up and down. Down and up. Up and down. I recognized it in my cells. I was the grape and the grape was me. And I knew, when the bubbles were all gone and the 7-Up went flat, I would be dead.

The dead part didn't trouble me in the least as I was predisposed to a certain morbidity back then, but the rising and falling part made me frankly ecstatic. I leapt up, glass in hand. I had discovered the meaning of life, or at least the meaning of *my* life.

*

Before I was medicated, I was a *rapid cycler*. My moods were volatile and my writing reflected that.

I wrote poems in pairs. The first effort was always something born out of despair, belabored and wrenched tearfully onto the page. As soon as it was done and I could hold that freshly inked paper in my hand, the success of the form outweighed the heartache of the content and I soared. I'd get so high that I'd promptly whoop out a second poem, inevitably a polar opposite to the first.

In the hospital, I was still clutching those poems. While the doctors distracted themselves, testing me and spewing multitudes of theories, the techs, patient with my obsession, said that what I wrote was diagnosable. My bipolar brain chemistry was manifesting as poetry. So they helped me weasel a typewriter into the ward.

*

I've always been a bit of a zealot about writing. At ten, when I was also a zealot about Christianity and bowling, things got pretty bad. I wrote poems about how I wanted God to correct my hook.

*

At twenty, by the time I got the results of my EEG and was diagnosed with temporal-lobe epilepsy, God was long dead to me. Nonetheless, I was protective of all the spiritual auras I felt, so when the neurologist explained to me that the extreme ecstatic states I sometimes reached were seizures, I was devastated.

God, whom I denied but sometimes felt, had been turned into an electrical impulse, and with Him went language: "In the beginning was the Word." I learned that hypergraphia can be a sign of temporal-lobe seizures. Everything mysterious and beautiful was becoming clinical. Each spike and dip on the great print out of my brain was charted and interpreted and reported to doctors who quickly became determined to medicate away my altered states.

*

The first seizure drug was like my third serious relationship.

It nearly killed me.

Things started off innocuously enough. The doctor said, "This pill will make it so you don't smell the images on TV anymore." Or that's what I heard. My sensory life was a bit out of whack. I had visual and auditory hallucinations and was plagued with smells that no one else could perceive. And I was suicidal.

I thought that pill would cure me.

Instead, after only a month, when I took a routine follow-up blood test, the result was that I got called into the neuro's office. He said, word for gregarious word, "Your body has quit producing white blood cells. You might die."

Ten years later, I asked my shrink for my chart. When I got it, that adverse reaction was summed up in one line: "Patient experienced Leukopenia on Tegretol."

It didn't say what I'd have said: *The drug the patient was taking so she wouldn't off herself nearly killed her, the irony of which thrust her into such a profound despair that she didn't eat for two weeks, though she went ahead and took her iron pills on an empty stomach, because the blood test had also shown that she'd become anemic, and she still, stubbornly, wanted to believe that pills would make things better.*

Now I'd say my bone marrow was depressed, literally.

*

After I recovered from the first drug, the neurologist told me if I didn't take *some* medicine, I'd end up brain damaged. It seemed like a ploy to make me behave. I started taking lovers instead of medication. Sometimes sex is better than a sleeping pill. Sometimes it's not. I went back to pills.

*

What's funny is how my love of language and metaphor doesn't translate into the ability to understand the linguistic aptitude tests the medical community dishes out.

I don't know how many times I've been pretty coherent but ended up confounded by something that I know is trite. At my disability hearing, the psychologist asked me to explain the meaning of the expression: "We'll cross that bridge when we come to it."

I pictured a ravine, a deep ravine. I imagined that I desired to cross it but was thwarted by steep cliffs. I told the doctor, "I'll keep walking until I find a bridge."

They labeled me "Unfit to work."
"Unfit to write" was not implied.

*

I got accused of plagiarism in eighth grade. It was my content more than any particular proficiency with language that sparked the rebuke. I'd written about war, about "bedraggled" poppies manifesting the spilled blood that was still rising in the German landscape (where I had lived before I moved to New Mexico).

I tried to fight the slander but no one would believe the poem was mine.

I quit talking.

Actually I quit talking and I quit bathing. In short order, my parents traipsed me off to my very first head doctor, the church counselor. Looking back, it amuses (and horrifies) me that a literary battle served as the catalyst for my indoctrination into the mental-health system.

*

As an adult, when I'd become known as a local writer, a middle-school teacher came to me with a poem by a sixth grade girl and asked, "Is this plagiarized?"

I read the poem. It was beautiful and I knew that here in this small sonnet was my vindication. I turned to the teacher and said, "No. She's simply thinking."

*

In my mid-twenties I wrote a sonnet when I was manic. It was one of those nights plagued by insomnia where I'd been writing for ten hours. Finally, near dawn, I reread the poem and found it to be stunning. Then it hit me, "It's Shakespeare."

I deleted it.

Then I doubted.

I still doubt.

*

The intersection of writing and mental health is often quite literal.

I can look at samples of my writing and often know what medication I was on (or not taking) by the grammatical constructs. Unmedicated, I am the perpetual epiphany. In turn, most of the antipsychotics leave me flat, clutching reality as if spelling out the word "s-e-c-u-r-i-t-y." Exaggerated manias or depressions showed up alternately as run-ons or fragments. Perhaps to another person, lots of the non-effectual drugs made for less than particularly coherent writing.

And then there is subject matter. There was a ninety-page novel I whipped out at nineteen in preparation for going on Lithium. It was called *The Zookeeper* and the animal I was hoping to tame was in my brain, digging so persistently that debris was piling up in my lungs. (I swear you can't breathe properly when depressed; the whole world, even the air is shallow.) When they wouldn't let me go on Lithium because my EEG was abnormal, I threw the novel out.

In my twenties I wrote another medicinal novel. This one had a contemporary woman with an imaginary hero called "Doctorman." (Doctorman was based loosely on Weir Mitchell, the doctor who developed the rest cure to treat hysterics.) And the woman in the novel wanted to be "the good patient." (She was modeled after Charlotte Perkins Gillman, hysteric and author of "The Yellow Wallpaper.") She would even hold her hair out of the way while Doctorman marked up her back with fruit-scented markers for an auditorium of rapt students and doctors.

"This spine," he'd say, "is experienced as a veritable skewering onto the planet earth."

Interpreting a bizarre sensory experience caused by seizures as an opportunity to become grounded, at least in literature, helped me imagine some kind of peace.

*

I'm not supposed to be creative. There's a test for that too and I've failed it. In middle school as part of a battery of examinations for an I.Q. test, I was given a piece of paper with an empty grid consisting of sixteen boxes. I was instructed to fill in all the boxes with drawings. I suspect what they were looking for was range and variety, and by that, they thought they could gauge creativity.

My very practical brother had to take the test too and was deemed highly creative for offering up renditions of all the lamps and chairs and pencil holders in the room.

What I gave them was sixteen pictures of jellyfish.

Jellyfish seen from above, jellyfish from below, jellyfish from the side. Little jellyfish, big jellyfish. Jellyfish in all their myriad manifestations of shape and tentacle.

I'd just come back from Virginia where I'd been out in the Atlantic on my uncle's fishing boat. I'd spent the entire boat ride staring into that jelly-riddled water and fervently ignoring everything my brother caught and how it smelled. I'd come back to the desert with one thing on my mind: jellyfish.

What the counselors failed to recognize was my appreciation of subtle variety.

Now I think they could have looked at that drawing and diagnosed me with *Obsessive Compulsive Disorder,* or at least as the child of a father with OCD.

I don't have OCD, but I have tendencies.

I don't mind.

Obsessiveness, often underestimated, can also manifest as persistence.

A decade later, when I was in my pamphleteering, garage-bookmaking phase, I named one of my pseudo presses 16 *Jellyfish Publications*.

*

I didn't quite test up to Mensa snuff, but when my shrink of ten years finally got a hold of the three digits in my I.Q., she summed up my whole life and all our interactions with two words: "No wonder."

I was horrified.

No wonder what?

Intelligent people have problems living in civilization?

*

My medical chart is big, almost Proustian. Those manila folders are fat with interpretations of my life. Most of the time I hate the fact that someone else is trying to tell my story. I even hate the documentation of despair. However, when I applied for Social Security Disability, it helped to have all those sad songs spelled out in technicolor.

Usually people diagnosed as bipolar don't qualify for Disability the first go round, but I did.

Two things mattered: my chart and my writing. The doctors played their part, but when I filled out the book of forms asking about my life, I knew how to articulate what it was like for me to try to juggle my tumultuous brain. For example, I (truthfully) defined my attention span as ranging from less than a complete sentence to sixteen hours. I even told them I was in the middle of writing a book. Then I told them it was poetry.

I got the assistance.

Since I've been on Disability, all kinds of things have happened to make my chart even fatter. Yet, the medical industry's textualization of my life is rivaled by what I write.

And I write a lot.

And I've been coherent lately. Or at least I write my way into coherence. Some of my doctors don't even think I'm bipolar anymore. But, after an NEA fellowship and two books (which I foisted upon them), they all know I'm a poet. They also know that no matter what they write down in my chart, I'm going to turn around and tell my own version of the story. The coroner may get the last word, but I'll have my say until then.

The voice of the intellect is a soft one, but it does not rest until it has gained a hearing. Ultimately, after endlessly repeated rebuffs, it succeeds. This is one of the few points in which [we] may be optimistic about the future of mankind. . . .

SIGMUND FREUD
The Future of an Illusion
1927

Woe to you, my Princess, when I come you shall see who is the stronger, a gentle girl who doesn't eat enough or a big wild man who has cocaine in his body.

SIGMUND FREUD
letter to his fiancée,
Martha Bernays
1884

1 Interpersonal Arghing

an exploration of violence in adult life

1:1   In 2003 I threatened to hold up the MRI clinic.

I went to the ER and told them
my legs had been numb for five weeks.
They told me to eat mandarin oranges.

They told me to eat mandarin oranges
and then shrugged, as if legs didn't matter.

So I threatened to hold up the MRI clinic.
Self-preservation is instinct.

I needed to know what was going on.
I needed to know what to do.

I knew: legs matter. (Sometimes
logic prevails.) So I got my hands
on an old sawed-off shotgun and

I threatened to hold up the MRI clinic.

1:2   You want to know where the shotgun came from?

It came from my knee—
this was a weapon birthed from patella and ligament,
hard-hitting myth born the day I decided
I would not leave a man's hands wrapped around my windpipe.

It took years to get around to defending myself,
it took less than a minute without oxygen

as if my head had been forced underwater in the River Styx
fish swimming by

a baptism into adrenaline
fast riddle of flesh
this time the answer was a leg.

I rammed my knee into the soft tissues of his belly
and forced that man's body from mine.

Like that—I was breathing again
and only the sky was blue.

1:3   Things are not always so simple.
       Sometimes logic prevails.

       Once I carried a man
       out of the bedroom
       he'd cornered me in.

       I carried him down the stairs
       through the hallway
       and dropped him on the doorstep.

       On the actual threshold.

       I wanted to *unmarry*
       the moment of our meeting
       so I picked him up

       much the same way
       he'd picked me up—
       with a sentence.

       I bet him I could
       carry him down the stairs.

I bet him I could
carry him down the stairs
when all my usual means

of getting a guy off
me were failing.
It was so mundane

so plain and unimaginative
—the accosting—
pedantic and cloying,

the buttons on my pants
pulled
repeatedly apart.

I gave him back ritual.
I gave him story.
I gave him the time it took
to get to the door.

       And then I ran.
Just in case.

1:4   In case
       you were wondering,
       reciprocity matters to me.

       The time someone left a tooth
       in the back seat of my car after a break-in
       was somehow more creepy and more meaningful
       than the usual rock through my window.

       I thought of the tooth fairy.
       I thought of payback.
       I thought of justice.

       Fair's fair.
       Sometimes.

       At least I hold up my end of deals,
       try to give back better than I get.

1:5   I got mandarin oranges at the ER.
Sometimes logic doesn't prevail.

I told them my legs had been numb for five weeks.
Six hours later, they gave me a little plastic container

of hump-backed wedges.

The fruit tasted like straw.
The fruit tasted like the last straw.

So sweet, so orange—it went to my blood.

Okay, I thought, *Keep me from fainting.*
Keep me on my numb feet.
Give me the energy to figure out what to do.

1:6   I get tired of the onslaught.

One man threw a blanket over my head.
If he hadn't been shoving his knee into my crotch
and his tongue into my mouth, I would have gone to sleep.

It's so old, the harassment.

When I have insomnia, I can't count how many times
I've been followed or stalked or felt up or groped
or slapped or flashed or propositioned or catcalled
or had a gun pulled on me . . . no, I can count that.

Once.

Once a man pulled out a pistol
and began gesticulating at me.

I knew him and although I wasn't entirely sure
what he had in his hands, it looked like a .22 caliber
bluff.

He wanted to sleep with me.

(Ten minutes before, he'd made me feel his bicep,
told me how hard it was to resist punching doors.)

I ran.
It was beautiful—not getting shot.

1:7   I can fathom beauty,
      still,
      and that's not the half of it.

      I eat apricots
      and let my lover hold me.

      This lover.
      This time.

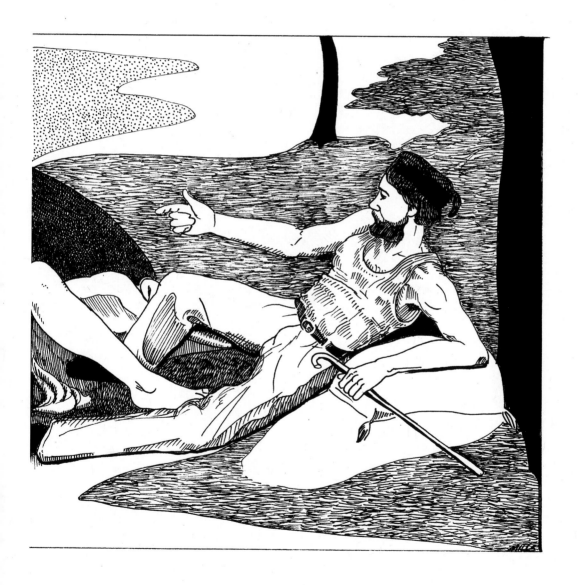

1:8   The man who tried to choke me
was also a lover.

I didn't hurt him until
we had been together nine months.

A full term of knockdowns.

He was simply escalating
but I was taking the necessary time
to birth self-preservation.

Reciprocity matters.
But so does integrity.

He said he loved me.
For a long time I just loved him back.

That was the miscarriage.
My knee was something else.

1:9   The shotgun was already in my possession
months before I went to the ER with numb legs.
I'd gotten the gun when a man posing as the propane guy
poked around my property and wedged himself
into my entryway, scoping me and the place out.
I knew he'd figured out that I live alone. I also knew,
if he came back, he'd figure out I have a shotgun.

1:10   A body part.

A body part
present part past.

Conglomerate of muscle
memory and skeleton.

Thin skin of contentment.

Story eking out a fragile
existence between the unspeakable
and the forgotten.

Did I tell you
I love life?

I go barefoot in the Rio Grande,
blue sky overhead.

1:11   Underneath everything,
there's shame.

It's a question of complicity.

I did what I had to do to survive.
Is that wrong? Or "less than" the untested?

Know: Self-preservation is instinct.
      Sometimes it kicks in.
      And sometimes it is not
      so recognizable
      as a fist.

1:12   Violence does funny things to the brain.

You learn fear.
You learn primal.
You learn choice and lack of choice.

You learn that a man's hand will fit around
your entire bicep like a vice, the screw tightening
one phalange at a time.

One man took me that way.
Dragged me off.
I didn't fight.

Sometimes logic prevails.
If I didn't want the shit beaten out of me by a boxer,
then I had to succumb.

1:13   But I didn't have to stay in my body.

I left.

I went to Salisbury and climbed into the eye of a chalk horse.

I went to London and ate apricots by the Thames.

I took a ferry from Dover to Calais
and bought marbles.

I didn't lose any until I got back

to that motel room

on Central

and found a man climbing off of me.

1:14 I climbed to the top of the Zügspitz
when I was a child.

By myself.

It was magnificent,
the peak
of childhood.

Actually I took a train
followed by a tram
and then walked into the café full of skiers
and ordered hot chocolate.

Nobody knew where I was.

It was terrifying.
I was ten and my German
was kaput and my French limited
to numbers and a few schoolyard slurs.
I was afraid I'd get lost on the mountain.
I was afraid I'd need to ask for help
and lack the language.

1:15 At the ER, I told them I used to be a runner.
I was good.
I didn't mention what I'd run from.

I just told them that five weeks prior
I'd been hiking six miles a day.

And then I told them
crossing my kitchen shouldn't feel like crossing
the Rubicon.

1:16   In *almost* everything,
there's one cutting differentiation.

I was not the predator.

You salvage what you can
from the razor's edge of memory.

1:17   Remember: violence is systemic.

I am not the only woman combing through the dregs
to cull a life that can be called thriving.

Survival is just the beginning.

Violence does funny things to the brain
and the brain manhandles memory.

Picture a red crest of everything at once.

Silence makes it swell. Speech makes it abate
a bit. Language offers the possibility of putting things

in their places: forefront, backburner.

You have to deal with trauma before you can
let it go the way of the past.

You have to hold the culture accountable.

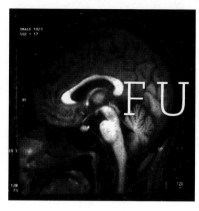

FUSE

I was reaching for a carton of milk when the boxer who raped me four years prior walked up and said, "Do you remember me?"

Homogenized. Two percent. Fat free. Or whole.

I slowly picked a carton from the shelf, turned, and looked him square in the eye.

"Yes," I said, "I remember you."

I didn't even drop the milk.

I'd expected him to show up again one day. Actually I expected him every day. Nonetheless, when he did finally appear, I was stunned, so stunned that it took me hours to venture out of the grocery store, hours which became a blur of label-reading and adrenaline. I never returned to that store again.

*

One of my friends got roses from her rapist.

For months after the event, he sent one bright red dozen to her house each week. She was still in high school and hadn't told her parents what happened. They encouraged her to accept the attention of this slightly older, obviously well-to-do young man.

I never trusted flowers after hearing her story. My mistrust was validated several years later when I received both the largest floral arrangement I'll ever get before death *and* an ultimatum: *sleep with me or else.*

That was from a professor.

The answer, for once, was easy: I dropped out of the program.

*

I always knew I'd get raped.

I can't tell you how I knew, but I knew. And I never doubt my epiphanies. As soon as I was old enough to be culturally aware, I latched onto the statistics in lieu of any sort of explanation. One in four women will be victims of sexual assault in her lifetime with the largest window of rapes happening between age 16 and 24. (My home state of New Mexico is worse than most states.) I was determined not to have rape be my first sexual experience. I'd seen what it had done to my friend: she'd lost her ability to say *No* to anyone. *No* had ceased to have any power. She didn't even try anymore. I'd argue, for years, with as many men as possible, that a cowering woman in a closet who's not capable of saying *No* is not giving an implicit *Yes*. There ought to be such a thing as discernment.

Nonetheless, I was afraid of living her story. My plan was to have sex first, before I was raped, and see if things could work out better.

*

So when I was eighteen going on nineteen, I was on the prowl.

I wanted to get it over with.

I found a boyfriend, settled into a groove, and then took his subtle advances as my opportunity and said, "Let's do it." He was game, at first. Then I let it slip that I'd never had sex before and he balked.

"You're drunk."

"It's okay. I really want to have sex."

"But you shouldn't be drunk your first time."

"But I really want to have sex."

"I shouldn't be drunk your first time."

"But we both want to."

"No, we're drunk."

"Are you seriously saying *No*?"

"Yes."

We had sex in the morning when we were hung-over. God, I was ecstatic. I'd done it. I was free. No matter what happened, my will was going to be mine and no one would be able to take that away.

*

A year later, the last thing my rapist said to me was, "You were my first."

It wasn't yet 7 o'clock in the morning. It was a Saturday in late summer. I was trying to get my clothes back on. His *first*? His first what? Sexual experience? I tried to thread the loop to my wraparound skirt. His first *rape*? I couldn't feed the end. Then it hit me. I pulled the tie through the hole. He was black. I tied the knot. He meant his first *white* woman.

And then he added, "Just like I expected."

Up until that moment, I'd simply been what he'd treated me as: an orifice, an orifice with legs that were in the way. The sound of him yelling "wider" would echo for years. After he spoke, I became a white woman with an orifice. That's how I got on the bus, a white woman with an orifice and a question: "Was it rape or race relations?"

If it was race relations, I'd failed: I left my body. I couldn't remember anything between when he forced my legs out of the way and when he climbed off of me. I doubt I even twitched I was so far gone from the threats and impending violence.

If it was rape, I'd failed, too: I didn't fight back.

*

Not long after that, about a year later, I did try to intervene in a domestic violence situation. From a second story apartment, I saw a man on the first floor kick a woman in the face and knock her down. It was the kind of kick where teeth get lost. My boyfriend got on the phone to the cops and I gave the play by play:

"She's on the ground . . . he's kicking her in the stomach . . . she's trying to get up . . . oh God. . . ."

He had her pinned and was choking her. I was out the door, my boyfriend following me. Another tenant from the complex was also running down. The man stood up when we got there, and said, to us, "Where's my fucking dog?"

His boots had her blood on them and yet he said it again, "Where's my fucking dog?"

The woman started crawling into the house. There was broken pottery all over from a plant that had gotten kicked. Then he yelled it at her, "Where's my fucking dog, bitch?" and as soon as he moved towards her, we grabbed him. All three of us. I took a bicep. I threw my whole weight into it. I felt like a 5-foot 10-inch 110-pound piece of tinsel on his arm, but it was working. We kept him outside while she got the door shut and locked.

Then he shook us, muttered some more about the dog, and stormed out the back gate to his motorcycle and rode off. When the cops finally got there, we told them what had happened, and then the woman told them that we were hiding the guy. An hour after that, it was clear she wouldn't press charges. By the next morning, I had the scoop from neighbors: this was regular. "Didn't you notice her limp?" By the next week, the front window was busted out and they disappeared.

My heart broke. I took a self-defense class.

*

I've never had a black eye but my next lover knocked me down. A lot. He'd pretend he was drunk and run into me, knock me to the floor. It didn't look like what I'd seen. I didn't put two and two together and call it domestic violence until he tried to kill me. I should rephrase that. He didn't try to kill me. He tried to show me that he *could* kill me. There's a difference. Funny how close it can get to death and still be distinct.

At first I thought the attack was a joke. Then I thought, "I can't breathe." Then, "He's supposed to love me." Then I realized it didn't matter if he was supposed to love me, I was going to die. I went blind with panic but I started fighting. My arms were pinned by his knees but I was able to strike him hard with a leg. When I got him off me, he didn't come back at me. There was no kicking me in the stomach or throwing me against the wall. It was just over.

He let me climb out of the bed, somehow get dressed and walk out the door. Of course, I don't remember that part, the leaving or where I went, I just remember every second of the fight.

I fought.

I actually fought back. That's the part that stuns me. That's the part that gives me hope. That's the part that's wound around my self-definition.

And I didn't go back.

Since then I've known: *I will do what I have to do.*

*

I started warning people not to mess with me *and* I started calling bluffs, in part because I never could quite forgive myself for giving in to the threats from my rapist. What came out of his mouth overpowered me emotionally, and then I confronted the fact that physically he was pure muscle while I was anorexic. The combination of his strength and my malnutrition had been deadly; I was so weak there was no way I could fight or break his grip. I'd learn that what happened fits under the legal definition of rape, but I can't help but think, *still*, that expecting to be raped didn't work to my advantage. Those years I was constantly a deer in headlights. I picture myself frozen.

I stayed frozen after the rape, didn't even tell anyone what happened for another ten years. And when I did finally speak, I said he was a boxer but I didn't say he was black. The idea that black men are after white women is a myth and I didn't want to coincidentally perpetuate it. (Statistically about 80% of rapes happen within the same race.) I did admit that he picked me because I had been hungry. He fed me a grilled cheese sandwich before he started threatening me. Afterwards, the fact that I'd eaten something he'd purchased made me feel like a whore. It took me a while to get over the eating disorder.

*

I heard through the grapevine that the man who tried to kill me got held up at gunpoint under a bridge the next year. He didn't get shot but did start having panic attacks. I was relieved. He needed to have a breakdown if he was ever going to have a chance at becoming human again. I cared about him and wanted that for him. Besides, the holdup with a gun mirrored what he'd done to me and I liked thinking that it was both good for him and repayment for what he'd done.

My continued survival against odds was proving that the universe would take care of me, and in turn, that people shouldn't fuck with me.

*

By the time I got hit head-on by a drunk driver at 31, I was even able to give testimony in court. I read a victim impact statement. He got the max.

It wasn't until they took him jump-suited and handcuffed away that I started crying. I wasn't a pretty sight. I never let on to anyone, but truthfully, I felt like I was in a movie and he was some kind of lover being parted from me.

An experience like a crash from opposite directions bonds you—especially when someone easily could have died. A few inches on the drunk driver's part and it could have been me. And if I hadn't fallen asleep and been late to pick up my friend (and consequently on time for the impact), the two people in the convertible behind me would have been dead.

In many ways, the drunk driver and I were perfect together.

When someone first yelled, "He's running!" all I felt was relief that he wasn't dead. Only later did I comprehend that he was trying to leave the scene. Onlookers caught up to him in the alley and beat him into submission. The cop told me. Nobody knew which of his wounds were from the car accident and which were from the fight. It wasn't until much later that I'd find out it was his third offense. He'd even had the lucidity to take all the registration and insurance papers with him when he ran.

Nobody let us speak on site, but I practically lived with him for a whole year afterwards. Everyday, my soft tissues and organs were aware of his impact, and every time I couldn't pick up fifty pounds of chicken feed or carry my own laundry, I remembered him. It was worse than a crush. The lap belt cinched my gut into some kind of twisted reverie.

In the courtroom, I knew what he'd done but I also knew what I was doing: helping sentence him. It didn't exactly feel good. When he went to prison, I toyed with the idea of writing him letters, but none of my friends or family would hear of it. Plus, I was still in physical therapy and I couldn't quite forget that my life *hadn't* flashed before my eyes, that if the crash *had* been fatal, my last thought would have been "maroon"— the color of his truck.

*

My current doctor thinks threatening to hold up the MRI clinic was simply a Post-Traumatic Stress Disorder [PTSD] reaction, but nothing's simple. Rapist, lover, asshole, drunk driver. By the time I was thirty-three, I knew I wanted to be the one to pop the question, "Do you remember me?"

"Do you

remember me?"

No man and woman have a right to bring into the world those who are to suffer from mental or physical affliction. It condemns the child to a life of misery and places upon the community the burden of caring for it, and probably for its defective descendants for many generations.

MARGARET SANGER
Woman and the New Race
1920

No woman can call herself free who does not own and control her body. . . . Against the State, against the Church, against the silence of the medical profession, against the whole machinery of dead institutions of the past, the woman of today arises.

MARGARET SANGER
"Shall We Break This Law?"
Birth Control Review
1917

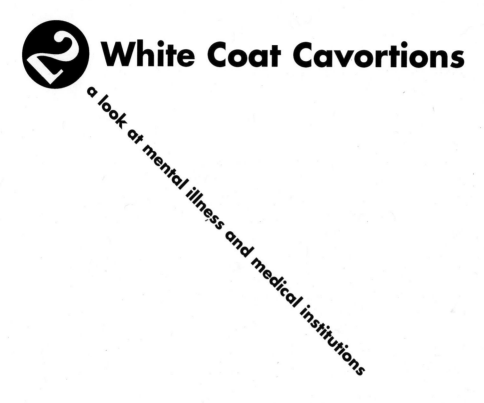

White Coat Cavortions

a look at mental illness and medical institutions

2:1   I threatened to hold up the MRI clinic.

My legs had been numb for five weeks.
I needed to know what was going on.
I needed to know what to do.

Self-preservation is instinct
so I left the mandarin oranges
and went to the mental hospital.

I told them I had a shotgun. I told them
I was going to hold up the MRI clinic.
I shot off my mouth and meant it.

They said, "But are you suicidal?"
As if
homicidal wasn't enough.

Self-preservation is instinct.
I thought of the holdup going awry
I thought of not getting my MRI
and then I said, "Sure . . .
sure, I'm suicidal."

I got locked up.
(Violence is institutionalized.)
I got locked up and drugged with antipsychotics.

All I wanted was a brain scan.
All I did was threaten
to hold up the MRI clinic with a shotgun.

2:2 You want to know where I got the shotgun?

I got the shotgun from a friend.

After ten years
he finally trusted me not to rig it
to a rope round a door
and blow my brains out.

It was beautiful.

A Brazilian 12-gauge.

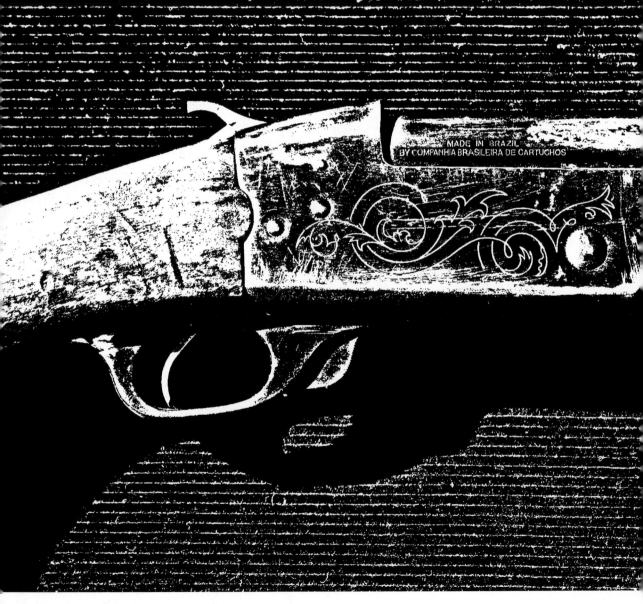

2:3   Back in 1990, it was too late to pump my stomach
so they put an IV into my arm
and said, "Were you trying to kill yourself?"

My lips were numb.
I tried to say, "No."
It came out, "Do you think I'm stupid?"

Self-preservation is instinct.
I'd only taken 15 pills and called for help
when my head went numb three hours later.

I knew: heads matter.

The pills were a red mistake.
Usually I could endure what happened.
I'd taken 30 white pills and been fine.

Once I'd even taken two of everything
in the house. A perversion of Noah's Ark.
I'd called Poison Control after

seventy pills. They said
"Can you vomit?"
I said, "Sure."

I hadn't had reason to suspect
15 pills would tether me to a hospital bed.
I told the doctors as much.

My head was a pincushion
but my mouth was something else—
a rubber stamp into the institution.

I got locked up.
It was "voluntary." They said,
if I didn't go, they'd commit me.

I thought of which way I'd get out faster.
Sometimes logic prevails.
I figured I'd lose seventy-two hours on the outside

if I was agreeable.

2:4   Five weeks. My legs had been numb for
five weeks when I went to the ER.

I'd already been to my primary.
She took X-rays.

They were clean as something else going on
so she gave me a referral to a neurologist.

I called every neurologist in the phonebook
trying to get an appointment.

I knew: crossing my kitchen
shouldn't feel like crossing the Rubicon

and I'd fallen
for the idea that someone might help me

this time. I knew:
I wasn't crazy.

The numbness was more stable
than anything in my life.

So I called every neurologist in the phonebook
trying to get an appointment.

The earliest they could see me
was three months.

I knew: I couldn't wait.
Legs matter.

So I went to the ER.
They gave me mandarin oranges.

2:5   I haven't given the doctors any fruit baskets
        but I haven't given them the easiest time
        either. My symptoms were odd
        or confounding.

        I passed out whenever I was cornered.
        I lost my vision when anything approached my face.
        I could feel air where my wrists should be.

        I saw bats
        and heard bells
        and felt my spine like a skewer.

        I didn't sleep.
        I gave my money away to strangers.
        I hurt myself.

2:6   I gave myself a worse time
        than anyone else would ever be capable of.

        Or that's what I hoped
                when I held a cigarette to my arm
                when I quit eating
                when I overdosed
                when I put a blade into my wrist.

        Self-preservation is instinct
        but sometimes logic prevails.
        To survive I had to preserve some semblance
        of power.

2:7   To survive
I had to get help.

I saw my first shrink at twelve,
my second at fifteen,
my third at eighteen
my fourth at nineteen
and my first neurologist at twenty.

The first shrink said manic depressive and wished me well.
The second shrink said I was a problem and threatened to lock me up.
The third said bipolar and gave me an antidepressant.
The fourth called me schizoaffective and gave me antipsychotics.

The neurologist said, Hmmm,
and hooked
so many wires to my scalp
I felt like Medusa.

Nobody turned to stone.

My brainwaves lapped (the auditory hallucinations)
over the parameters of normal (the visions)
and spilled into the territory (the strange smells)
of temporal lobe seizures (stranger sensations).
For a while, (the déjà vus)
I thought everything made sense.

2:8   I'd fallen for the idea that someone might help me.
I'd fallen for the idea that pills might help.
The first seizure drug didn't seem to be doing much.
Then the doctor called me in after he got the results
of a blood test and said, "Your body has quit
producing white blood cells. You might die."

I was twenty.

Nobody had warned me that there could be fatal
side effects. It seemed like something
they should have said
since there were
statistics.

Then he said, "You might recover."

2:9   I didn't particularly expect to live
but *might, maybe, possibly, if you're lucky,*
I did.

I recovered enough to try another drug.

It triggered seizures
but the doctors assumed I was just hyperventilating
because I was hysterical
so they put me on sedatives.

When I kept getting worse,
they realized it was a reaction to the second drug
and took me off everything.

And put me on a third drug
that treated both seizures and bipolar disorder.

I stayed on that drug for eight years.

It helped some of my symptoms but was a bane
to my credibility.

The first thing any doctor wants to know
is what meds you're on and what you're allergic to.

Chink.

You're no longer a person with a physical problem.
You're a mental case.

2:10   I was out of the first hospital but still on
head drugs when my arm went numb
and I had to see my second neurologist.

I very calmly told the frat boy
in a white lab coat
that I couldn't feel my arm.

And then I told him that
arms matter,
that I typed a lot for my job

that my primary doctor thought
it might be carpal tunnel.
(I didn't say

that she'd first called my shrink
to see if
she could believe me.)

But he flipped

through my whole chart
until he came to
a diagram of my cervix
and then he said:

"Have you ever been tied up during sex?
Are you into S&M?
Do you like it rough?"

I stood up and started screaming.

The nurse ran in
and looked at me like I was crazy
and I knew: my word wouldn't count

against his.

So I ran.
I ran. Before they could catch me
and lock me up I was down the stairs

and out the door.
The sky was blue and I knew:
I'd gotten away

and that was all.

2:11   It's not always so easy to run.

Sometimes you're tethered to an IV.
Sometimes you're drugged with antipsychotics.
Sometimes your feet are in stirrups.

Or, your legs are numb
and you've fallen
for the idea someone might help you.

2:12   My feet were in the stirrups
for a routine gyn exam
when one doctor suddenly said to me,

"You have such a pretty cervix."

She was sincere.

2:13   At thirty, I couldn't even convince another doctor
that I knew whether or not I'd had sex, whether
or not I might be pregnant. I'd gone in for back
pain. He did a gyn exam and tests I told him
I didn't need. Of course, the results were negative.

2:14   At first in the ER, I was told that given my symptoms
they'd need to run a lot of tests.

I was relieved.
My legs had been numb for five weeks.

I'd gone from hiking six miles a day
to struggling to walk fifty yards.

I knew: crossing my kitchen
shouldn't feel like crossing the Rubicon.

And I'd fallen
for the idea someone might help me this time.

Then the doctors looked at my chart,
at the meds I take, the labels I've been given

and they told me it was all in my head.
I'd been online, I knew:

it probably was all in my head—literally.
That's why I needed a brain scan.

I mentioned lesions, mentioned an MRI,
but they just shrugged

and gave me mandarin oranges.
So I threatened to hold up the MRI clinic

and I got locked up. I got locked up
and drugged with antipsychotics.

hey wante

o they too

ll the drug

2:15 The first hospital in 1990 was a dream:

They wanted to diagnose me
so they took me off
all the drugs
to see what happened.

see wh

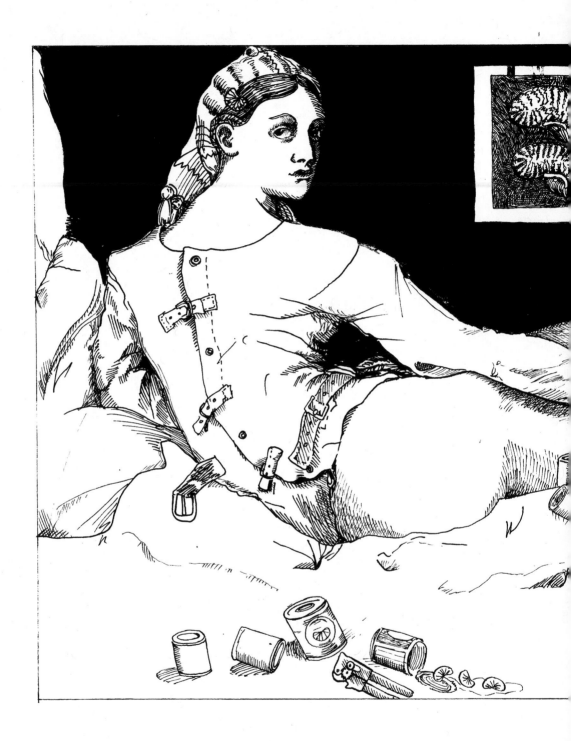

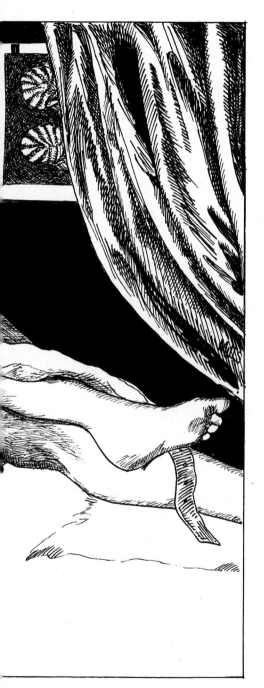

I was lucid for the duration.

I was lucid enough to listen
when older women told me
which men on the unit were predators.

They didn't mention any doctors
so I began to feel safe
as if I could open up.

2:16   I was locked up for five weeks.

I looked at ink blots.
I told stories.
I drew pictures.
I filled in bubbles.
I went to specialists.
I answered questions.
I started eating again.
I started getting stronger.

Some of it was a dream.
My symptoms were finally being taken seriously.
Some of it was something else.

2:17   I told one psychologist on the ward
that I'd overdosed in part because
whenever I tried to be intimate
with my boyfriend I had flashbacks
of four-foot-large male genitalia
that blocked out everything else.

Or, I saw a single quarter
being inserted into the flesh
of my arm as if I were a juke box
about to be played.

He said, "So you're a prude."

It was devastating. At first.

Then I burned my arm on a smoke break
and something snapped.

2:18   The epiphany had started on the way to the ward.
They gave me time to go home and get my stuff,
time enough to off myself and I considered it

but self-preservation is instinct

so I packed my bag and went to say goodbye
to my boyfriend. We sat on the stoop outside
his apartment and I told him what I'd done: the pills
and what was happening: the hospital.

His face dropped.
Like a stone.

I saw it drop.

And I knew
for the first time
that hurting myself
hurt something more
than my own body.

2:19   When the psychologist said, "So you're a prude."
Something snapped.
Or it snapped when I burned my arm two hours later.

In that hole in my flesh,
I could see who was doing what.
I could link my own behavior to anger
and for the first time I saw another option.

Retaliation:
        I wrote a letter. I indicted the doctor's
        diction and called his version
        of listening a travesty, said no
        way was I going to be in the same
        room with that psychologist again.

The staff shook their heads as if
I was crazy
but they did get me a new psych.

2:20   The new psychologist said,
"You test schizophrenic,
but given everything,
we think it's Post-Traumatic
Stress Disorder. Do you know
who abused you in childhood?"

I was twenty. I had distorted flashbacks.
I said no

so they asked my parents.

2:21   I asked the doctors why I was the one locked up
when I was not the predator.

They had their reasons.
They had their pills in a cup
and bed checks.
They had restraints and syringes
filled with Thorazine.

2:22   The second time I was hospitalized,
a decade later,
intake was rough.

The nurse couldn't get a vein.
I was dehydrated.
She tried repeatedly in my arm
and then went for my hand.
She missed.
Pain seared something into my memory:

Mental wards do physicals.

2:23   I'm not afraid of the mental hospital.
You get a cigarette at the top of every hour.
You get meals and a bed.
You don't have to pretend
everything's okay.

2:24   I'm afraid of what happens
when you get *out*
of the mental hospital.

Of stigma.
Of being marginalized.
Of what happens when your voice doesn't count.

2:25   The only way I can explain
         what one doctor did to me

         (Violence is institutionalized.)

         is that maybe she wanted to
         take away my ability to carry

         a child.

         Or perhaps she was just sadistic.

         My pap smear had been normal and
         I had no symptoms
         but I was fresh out of the mental hospital

         so she said something was wrong with me

         and then under the auspices of a biopsy
         she went after my cervix.

I was fresh out of the mental hospital.
I did the only thing I could do.
I bled.

I projectile bled from my cervix
to her white lab coat.

She was horrified,
not at what she'd done to me
but that she'd gotten dirty.

(Sometimes the only vindication
for an abuse of power or justice
is to bleed very well.

Which I did.)

2:26   For months, I healed, slowly.
Other doctors peered and pondered
and called in specialists.

Nobody mouthed the word "malpractice."
Nobody said "crime."

I healed, slowly, and then one day
a few years later in a routine gyn exam
the doctor suddenly said,

"You have such a pretty cervix."

Of course, I thought. It's practically
brand new.

2:27   Did I tell you I love life?

For years I didn't even have medical insurance
so one shrink kept my meds stocked with free samples.

And the time I was working construction
and a piece of wood scratched my cornea,
a friend drove me to Urgent Care.

2:28   When I threatened to hold up the MRI clinic,
        I wanted to get locked up.

        I wanted them to take my shoelaces
        and my earrings and my lighter.
        I wanted them to lead me into another room
        and tell me to strip so they could look
        for wounds. I wanted them to draw blood
        and ask if I had any physical complaints
        so I could say "Yes! My legs are numb!"
        and they could call a consult who'd call
        a neurologist who'd get me an MRI.

        Understand: sometimes logic prevails.

        Even bladder infections
        can contribute to the crazies.
        On the ward, they know you can't treat
        a person's mental health when there is
        an underlying physical concern.

        And I thought, I hoped, that on the ward
        they could discern the difference
        between *desperate* and *crazy*.

DID I TELL YOU I LOVE LIFE!!?

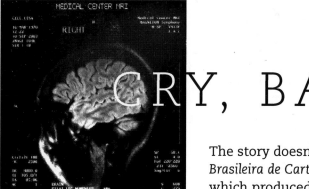

CRY, BABY

The story doesn't start with the *Companhia Brasileira de Cartuchos*—some factory in Brazil which produced a shotgun that would later have a hacksaw taken to it in America.

The story starts with my tear ducts on November 9, 1970 when I was eight months old. My tear ducts got clogged from an infection and I couldn't cry. I needed surgery, but when my mother took me to the hospital, I had a fever. The fever meant they couldn't use anesthesia. The doctor decided to do the surgery anyway, just without anesthesia. The nurse tightly swaddled me in blankets to restrain my arms and then Dr. Lichtig slid a skinny wire into one of my tear ducts. After he pulled it out, the nurse put a dropperful of dye into my eye and stuffed pieces of cotton balls up my nose. Then they did the other eye. Only when both cotton balls turned purple did he stop with the wire.

I don't remember that; the whole thing's gone the way of the middle of the rape and the aftermath of strangulation. Amnesia has its upside; I don't have to be conscious of all the yuck. Nowadays I suspect my body remembers everything, that my initial helplessness is rooted deep in my cells, but that was the era when traumas weren't supposed to affect babies. In that light, it's nothing but a story my mom tells every few years.

Finally, I asked her, "Did I cry?"

"Oh you screamed bloody murder. . . . I thought I was going to pass out."

Thirty-two years later, she sat with me in the ER as I tried *not* to cry.

Two days after that, I sat with a Brazilian

12-gauge on my kitchen table. It had a mahogany stock, was a single shot with take down action, and had a purfling metal design that reminded me of the engravings on musical instruments. The barrel and butt were sawed off. The whole thing would fit up a sleeve.

I made a decision.

*

The week before I looked from my legs to the nerve chart on my table and back to my legs. It was clear to me. The numbness had started with L-5 (lumbar) four weeks ago. Now I was numb to T-7 (thoracic).

I imagined mapping nerve paths onto my body. From sensation and lack of sensation, I knew exactly how each dermatome went. Nobody should ever have to know that information but since I did, I pictured doing it up right. I wanted to draw sharp black lines delineating the arcing shapes, which I would then fill with paint, color-coded to the date of onset. I imagined walking, or teetering, into the doctor's like a living paint-by-number anatomy text, handing them my body and a key to the color-coded time-line, and saying, politely, "Please, can you tell me what this means?"

I knew what it meant.

Googling had become a visceral activity. I'd research until I was shaking. I was beginning to understand; there were only a few official diagnoses possible according to the National Institute of Neurological Disorders and Stroke [NINDS] and only one of those sat in my brain squawking like a bird whose nest I'd come too close to.

Still, I wanted to be a good patient.

The same psychiatrist who'd thought my IQ was at the root of my problems had coached me to roll over with medical doctors. It seemed playing dumb was requisite to being a good patient.

And I knew I had to be a good patient if I was going to get any treatment.

And I needed treatment.

I wasn't even a good pedestrian anymore. Whatever was going on pulled my toes inward and scattered my center of gravity like breadcrumbs to pigeons.

I'd become a stumblebum, a teeterer, a total wobbler.

When the numbness started, I tried to catch my balance on the fly, in the middle of the fall. It wasn't long before balance was something to be created consciously. Standing in line at the check-out, I'd say, "Your legs are beneath you," and then I'd check. Carefully. Sometimes even turning my head was enough to knock me down as if my skull had gained momentum my body couldn't rival but the ground could.

Bonk.

If I was going to fall again in some public place, I wanted to fall into someone's arms. No, I wanted to fall into the arms of a neurologist.

*

Wriggle, flinch, cartwheel.

*

I went to the ER.

I went to the ER unpainted.

I took my Medicaid card and my mother and went quietly and calmly. I went prepared to play dumb. I signed in and when they called me, I recited my symptoms as if I were reading text from the side of a cereal box. I didn't feel the need to wave my arms around: these were serious symptoms.

It was unfortunate that I had to answer all the other questions, the ones that would plant seeds of doubt in the doctors' minds.

"Are you allergic to any medications?"

"I am only allergic to medications which prove something is organically wrong with my brain and my ability to present symptoms to you."

"What medications do you take?"

"I only take medications designed to alter a faulty brain, one predisposed to moods and obsessions, a brain which, if left unmedicated, would make presentation of physical complaints difficult."

"Oh, and you should know my insurance is based on poverty which gives you the right to make all kinds of assumptions."

Actually, the nurse paid attention to my symptoms, noted the medications I was on and what I couldn't take, and then left to meet with the doctor overseeing intake. Ten minutes later, the nurse returned, saying, "You're going to need a lot of tests. We want you to stay here and be seen in the ER."

"Okay," I said, the picture of compliance, a woman who could barely walk across the ER, saying, "Okay." Of course, that was just the holding tank phase of the game.

*

I was ushered back out to the waiting room where the channel was set permanently on distraction: cute animals playing. I sat by my mom and we watched the puppies and the goats for a while. Then a few tears rolled down my face. I knew I had to snuff them out, put a finger in the dam, or I wouldn't be listened to. I had to be calm and insistent, but nothing resembling histrionic. I had to get help.

I wanted the tests, but I didn't want the tests.

I would have preferred for the symptoms to suddenly evaporate in the waiting room, for all sensation to return, for weakness to recede. I would have loved to jump up and bound out the exit door, unhumiliated and free. I would have loved *not* to be begging for someone to tell me that life as I'd known it was over.

For six hours I alternately cried, held my mother's hand, and watched the animals playing. No one in the waiting room laughed out loud, but everyone seemed happy to stare at the set, as if forgetting whatever ailed them and drifting back into some pre-wounded reality, a reality where dogs and cats rollicked together and goats got into all the right things and didn't smell.

*

When my name was called I heard it like a siren song from beyond the ambulance bay. It was irresistible; it was a trap. I went anyways and they set me up in a curtained room.

I waited, a little calmer, figuring this should go smoothly.

My symptoms were classic: ascending numbness on both legs, weakness and balance problems, falls, as well as a slowed bowel and sped up bladder, plus I'd had temporary vision problems three months prior.

Truthfully, I'd had bizarre symptoms blown off a thousand times before, but I was sure this time would be different. There was no writing off legs.

And there was no writing *on* my legs.

I was the plain picture of restraint, unembellished and open to diagnosis.

When the resident came back he took my history and had me walk two steps, ignored the angle of my feet, then touched some instruments to my legs. I knew what a neurological exam should look like. This did not look like a neurological exam. This looked like some half-assed grab bag of excuses to dismiss.

"Well," he said, "Well, it's not Guillain-Barré because it's taken too long."

I knew it wasn't Guillain-Barré Syndrome, because the rising numbness had stopped at my hips, because if it was Guillain-Barré and I was having this much trouble getting treated, I'd be dead. I waited. When he said nothing, I said, "What about multiple sclerosis?"

"MS doesn't affect both sides of the body."

"Yes it does." I blurted, then said, "It can." I had articles and books in my bag which showed my symptoms as classic onset. I knew a lesion could sit across the spine and knock out both legs. I also knew lesions in the brain might theoretically reduce my impulse control and ability to deal with under-educated ER doctors.

"Do you have MS in the family?"

"No, but you don't have to have a genetic connection."

"Yes you do."

According to research, he was wrong. A theoretical argument, however, seemed pointless.

"So," I said, "You're going to do nothing? When I've gone from hiking mountains to barely making it across my house?"

"Well, you don't need a cat scan. We do CT's here."

I knew that also. "An MRI?" I prodded.

"A neurologist has to order an MRI. You need to see a neurologist."

"Yes I do, so . . . ?"

"I'll draw some blood and have my nurse give you a referral."

"Blood for what?"

*

The nurse said, "Your blood sugar has dropped so low, I'm going to get you some mandarin oranges and I want you to eat them before you try to leave. And here is the number to call to get a referral. Wait a week to give them a call and then they'll review your file and see if you need an appointment, and if you do, they'll schedule it within a few months."

"Did you say you want me to eat mandarin oranges?"

*

By the time my mom took me home, I was beyond despondent.

This was it.

Without steroids to waylay the flare, I was facing permanent damage, some or other degree of disability. So much for hiking. So much for living alone. So much for my plans of going back to work. Soon the handicap placard was coming to my car. Already I needed it but wanted to consider my situation temporary. With treatment I might be able to walk from regular parking lots to my destination again. Without treatment, even driving might end up out of the question. Already I was curbing myself because I couldn't feel the gas pedal or clutch, just pushed what was left of my legs into the memory of where things were.

*

So I got a ride to the mental hospital. When I finally got to see the intake nurse, I said, for the record, "My legs have been numb for five weeks. I need a brain scan. I have a shotgun and I'm going to hold up the MRI clinic."

"But why are you here?"

My bravado went poof, " . . . Because I want to hold up the MRI clinic?"

"Why not just go to the doctor?"

"I did. They dismissed me as crazy."

"So why are you here?"

"Because all I can think about is holding up the MRI clinic. . . ."

"Are you experiencing any delusions?"

"Well," I said, "I *thought* I got struck by lightning." To me this was the equivalent of saying I'd been struck down by God, but much later I realized I left out the God part.

"So?"

"I thought I got struck by lightning."

"Maybe you did."

"I doubt it. I was inside. I think it's neurological."

"When I was twenty-three, I got struck by lightning."

"*You* were struck by lightning?"

"I was out in a horse pasture, got thrown down, and blacked out for several hours."

"Mine wasn't like that. There was a flash in the sky while I was sitting in an armchair looking out the window. Then my arms started tingling as if I'd absorbed the charge," I said, then remembered why I was there, " . . . but a week later, my legs went numb."

And then we got into a conversation about her spinal stenosis. I can't remember her exact words, but what they conveyed to me was that her spine was disintegrating. I registered that she was being unprofessional, and also registered that if I pointed that out, I wasn't going to be viewed as a good prospective mental patient. Moreover, I was intrigued, torn actually, between needing to speak with someone who had some empathy, and the more pressing and urgent need to get diagnosed.

"I really need to be locked up," I told her.

"Okay, I'll let you talk to the doctor."

After I saw him, I met with her again.

"We don't have any beds here. Are you suicidal?"

"No beds?"

"There's another facility that might take you. Are you suicidal?"

"No," I said.

"Well, you have to be suicidal."

"But I'm threatening to hold up the MRI clinic . . ."

"But are you suicidal?"

Finally I got it, "Sure, yes."

"But when you talked to the doctor you said you weren't."

"I was mistaken. I am definitely suicidal."

"Okay, just make sure you say that you are suicidal—*use that word*—to the nurse at the hospital where we're sending you. Okay?"

*

So at the next facility, I said, *"Open sesame,"* and they locked me up.

*

When I told my cognitive behavioral therapist that I'd threatened to hold up the MRI clinic, he said, "I've found that when patients of mine need to see a neurologist at the ER, their best bet is to have a lawyer call and threaten the hospital."

I was stunned. It never occurred to me there was another option.

Then he said, "It's basically the same technique."

I was more stunned. How were legal wranglings and threats the same thing?

I flashed to the day he put a small finger puppet on his index finger. It was a little knit monkey with a little knit banana. "There's always a pay-off," he'd said. "There's got to be."

Then he'd blushed and put the finger puppet away.

The following week when I went for my appointment, I was still reeling with the idea that next time I went up against the medical industry I might be able to try a different approach. I asked him exactly what the lawyer needed to say.

"Malpractice," he said. "You have to get the Risk Assessment Team involved. Once the hospital lawyers are on it, the doctor's hands are tied."

. . . Research reveals a strong link between physical, sexual, and emotional mistreatment of children and the development of psychiatric problems. But in the early 1990s researchers thought of the damage as basically a software problem amenable to reprogramming via therapy or simply erasable through the exhortation, Get over it.

[However] such abuse, it seems, induces a cascade of molecular and neurobiological effects that irreversibly alter neural development. . . . We see the need to do much more to ensure that child abuse does not happen in the first place, because once these key brain alterations occur, there may be no going back.

MARTIN H. TEICHER
"Scars That Won't Heal:
The Neurobiology of
Child Abuse"
Scientific American
2002

Connecting the Polka Dots

the reckoning (13 lesions)

3:1   I threatened to hold up the MRI clinic.

Self-preservation is instinct
even for the intake nurse

so my threat got sawed off

much like the Brazilian 12-gauge
that is still in my closet.

Here's what you need to know:
it was a hack job.

I got locked up.
I got locked up and drugged
with antipsychotics.

The ward was a blessing.
The ward was a prayer.

After twenty-four hours
I was on my knees

wailing,
begging for an MRI.

The ward was a risk.
I didn't have the gun anymore.

3:2

The shotgun was never even loaded
with anything but metaphors.

I needed a neurologist to look at my brain
and check for lesions,

so I said "Here,
here is my backbone.
Today it is made of tropical wood
and steel and capable of blowing
a black hole in your skull."

I shot off my mouth and meant it
to be enough.

3:3   Nonetheless,
the on-call neurologist was scared of me.

I'd threatened to hold up the MRI clinic.

Usually I am a gentle woman, shy even
but I'm human, animal

and I liked his fear. I could smell it.
I could see it in his eyes.

I could flirt with it. I'd fallen
for the idea that I could dominate

the dialogue
without even raising my voice.

He ordered an MRI immediately.
It went swimmingly,

me stretched out in a tube daydreaming.
I already knew what they'd find—

my legs had been numb for five weeks
and my x-rays were clean as something else

going on—but right then I didn't care.
I'd gotten my way.

I'd gotten my MRI.

3:4   Polka dots.

They didn't say it,
but I knew when they ordered a spinal tap.

You don't feel like you have much of a backbone
when you're laid out on an examining table
under a drape with a hole cut to expose the space
between vertebrae where the needle will go in.

Here was my resignation.
My quiet whimper.
My big spine.

3:5   The moment he said Multiple Sclerosis,
I shrank.

Picture a girl on antipsychotics
in a heap on the floor of a mental ward.

From the floor, I said, "Can I see?"

I wanted to look at the MRI's.

I pictured spots,
ethereal ghost images,
blank spaces where my gray matter
should have been.

The neurologist just said, "It's definitely MS."

And I knew what I'd already figured out,
and I knew for sure why I'd fought,
and I wished I'd been wrong:

      Here was disease.
      Here were my numb legs.
      Here was the rest of my life curtailed.

"But you'll treat me?"
"Yes."

3:6   When I went back on the ward,
even the doctors and nurses cooed.

The patients were already sympathetic.
My legs had been numb for five weeks

so my response to the routine question
              "What are you in for?"
had stymied them from day one

as if legs
were somehow more real
than depression.

It was like the first hospital
where you got labeled
with an A or a B.
A's were addicts, addicts
were curable,
B's were something else.

It was worse than school.
Letters counted.

I wrote an elegy
for the addict
I could have been
considered.

No avail.
They wouldn't change my label.

Now I was a D.
Diseased.
Despondent.
Deplete of hope.

I thought perhaps I was in the wrong place.
Then they gave me steroids.

3:7   Steroids do funny things to the brain.

I woke up delighted
that I was so fucking smart

I could diagnose a neurological disorder
based on numbness that rose like a tide

from my toes to my hips.
Brain damage my ass.

Here was a head that could figure out
anything that mattered

like when and how to work the system
to get a brain scan

and everybody
in the world has to admit it—say it—

threatening to hold up the MRI clinic
was the smartest thing I've ever done

even if I got locked up
and who said lock-up wasn't bliss?

You get pudding
on your meal tray

You get pudding
and a cigarette at the top of every hour

and you know:
I'll beat this.

Numb legs or no
I can walk circles around the ward

or at least talk
circles because God help me

this is life
this is my fricking life

and I love it.

3:8   Then I crashed.

(Sometimes logic prevails.)

I'd fallen
for the third time in one day and
I couldn't believe it.

My legs were still numb.
Even my genitals were numb. (Numb genitals
do not make for a good mood.)

I cursed God.
I cursed a patient streaking down the hallway.
I asked the nurse *Why?*
Why me?
Hadn't I been through enough?

She shrugged and held out
a paper cup with a sedative.

I swallowed it.
I swallowed all of it
and went to bed.

I had no intention of ever getting up.

3:9   The sensation of one toe
coming back to life
woke me.

It hurt.

It was only the side
of one little pig
but it was enough.

The beginning of a resurrection.
A wiggling rejubilation.
I recanted everything

and got out of bed.

3:10   I got out of the hospital after almost a month
       when I was moonfaced and bloated from steroids
       when I could feel two toes on each foot
       when I could answer the question, "Will you
       get rid of the shotgun?" with a straight face.

       They sent me home with a slip of paper,
       an outtake plan that had a list of meds
       and appointments with a neurologist,
       and a physical therapist, a counselor, and
       a psychiatrist, and a case worker.

       They sent me home
       with a slip of paper that said "severe"
       next to the words "multiple sclerosis."

3:11   I went for the follow-up with the neuro one month later.

He asked which long term treatment I wanted.
I'd been researching MS, knew that I couldn't take
most of the meds because there was a risk of suicide
especially if you had a history of depression. There
was only one option for injections and I told him so.

I also knew that the tightness in my belly was spasticity
knew that the fatigue was MS lassitude,
and I knew which drugs to ask for.

The doctor cowtowed, practically
cowered. I realized the fling was over.
I didn't want a doctor who did everything I said
and gave me no input as to what was going on.

I wanted a neurologist who wasn't afraid
to set me off. I wanted a neurologist to tell me
the truth. I wanted a neurologist who didn't know
I'd threatened to hold up the MRI clinic.

I wanted to know what I was up against.
I wanted to see my brain.

3:12 Six months later, when I'd recovered feeling
in my legs, I met with a new neurologist.

She hit me with a hammer.
Repeatedly.
One leg flew into the sky, the other did nothing.
Bipolar reflexes.
Neither response was normal.

She struck a tuning fork and put it to my shin.
I was supposed to say when I couldn't feel it.
Instead my whole body started trembling.

She raised her eyebrows
so I told her about the time a sitar concert
had made me hear laughter
every time I bent my neck down.
I told her I'd learned to keep my head up.

Without hesitating,
she slapped my MRI's onto the light screen.
I didn't know what I was looking at.
I didn't know anything but I could see polka dots.
I trembled again.

She flipped
through the films pointing out thirteen—count them—thirteen lesions
and then stopped.

"Oh," she said,
"You have a black hole. That's a dead lesion,
one that's been inflamed repeatedly.
You're not early in the disease."

Then she flipped some more
stopped, pursed her lips, and said,
"Your corpus callosum is thinner than I'd like to see."

And she showed me the arc,
the strip of brain that connects the two hemispheres,
the strip of brain that should have been plump.

"So what does that mean?"

"That means you'll have trouble with memory."

"Which kind of memory" I said, trying to be calm.
"Long term or short?"

"All memory."

3:13   I remembered everything I'd forgotten.
>Names, telephone numbers, how to write the number 6,
>my keys, where I went after my lover tried to choke me,
>the insides of houses in childhood, whole years.

And then I remembered what I remembered.
>Catching the bus with semen running down my legs,
>the doctor covered in blood, not being able to breathe,
>my chart opened like porn on a neurologist's desk.

And then my new neurologist startled me.
She said,
>"Which is worse, your PTSD or the MS?"

Doctors never believe in PTSD, never
ask how I'm doing. Even the psychiatrist
I saw after I was first diagnosed blew it off
preferring to call me bipolar and drug me.

I wondered how PTSD had suddenly gained credibility.
My corpus callosum was still lit up.
A bridge between hemispheres.

3:14   I thought of the flashbacks, the dissociation, the nightmares
        and insomnia of PTSD. I thought of numbness, tremors, spasticity,
        and what might happen with MS.
                            And then I realized my legs
        were back from their foray into abandon, my balance
        freshly reacquired through physical therapy.

        "Do you mean right now? Right now, I'd have to say PTSD."

        That's what I said.
        I couldn't believe it.

3:15   I couldn't believe that six months after the diagnosis
of a chronic illness, I had to admit that it was still the same-
old same-old plaguing me, what had been haranguing
me since childhood.

My body as a rag doll.
My body as a puppet on someone's hand.
My body pinned and my mouth pried open and gagging.

A yellow shirt.
A chiaroscuro image
of some shudder shudder yuck.

A cramp.
A twitch.
An ache.

A grief so deep it's

out of body
out of sight
out of mind.

Fragments.
Pieces.

The muck.
The mire.
The partially remembered
and mostly forgotten.

3:16   Amnesia is a brick.

You know it's there.
You stumble on it daily.

A tactile absence,
an impinging void,
a teeming emptiness.

A rattle.

I have forgotten enough
to know the shape
of what happened.

3:17   The shape of my corpus callosum
is not normal.

It's belittled.
Diminished.
Lacking heft.

A look of concern
on my neurologist's face.

I looked it up.

I punched Pandora's Box
into the internet.

3:18   Hit me.
Slap me.
Pinch me.

Punch a time card.
The bridge between hemispheres
is still being constructed in the crib.

I read until I was shaking.
Then I read some more.

Research shows that if I were a boy,
neglect could interrupt the development
of the corpus callosum.

Research shows that for girls
the skinny is sexual abuse.

Get it?

The MRI is a crime scene photo.
It's proof.
It's an unfathomable interruption.

It's a confirmation
of a suspicion I tried to disbelieve:
something happened.

Something happened when I was little.

3:19   Something happened
when I threatened to hold up the MRI clinic.

Picture a girl jumping
into a river that will rise up over her head.

Picture a girl jumping
back into her own body.

I expected lesions.
What I got was something else.

3:20   I got no more than I already knew instinctively:
the shudder shudder yuck of molestation.

3:21   I got more than I'd bargained for:
an MRI is no cupful of mandarin oranges.

I hadn't known
that sexual abuse mattered in such a concrete way.
I'd bought into the cultural dismissal, the *hush-hush
pretend it didn't happen and everything'll be okay.*

Secretly, I'd thought, sure, it affected
my emotions, my behavior, my learned ability
to leave my body.

I never thought of structural
reasons for dissociation, never thought
amnesia was anything more than practical,
some kind of denial.

Now here it was,
a toll bridge
between the hemispheres of my brain.

3:22 A bridge that led to other questions,
other unexpected answers.

Like temporal lobe abnormalities,
the music, the visions, the strange
smells and stranger sensations, the déjà vus
something I'd attributed to some fall,
some head injury I'd forgotten
or underestimated.

Come to find out
imbalances in the temporal
lobes are also known to occur
as a result of sexual abuse.

Another piece of the puzzle
snapped into place.

As if my life was becoming
coherent.

Finally.

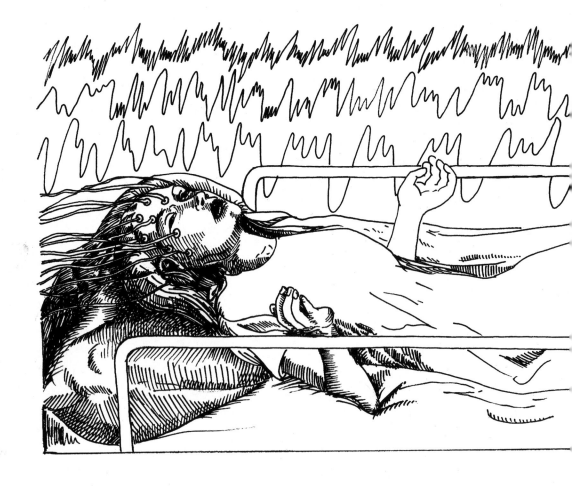

3:23   That day fifteen years prior
when I lay, wires on my scalp
as if I were Medusa, abnormal
electrical waves pouring out,
the writing was already on the wall
but nobody had read it.

Or at least not to me.

Perhaps the doctors had
turned to stone.

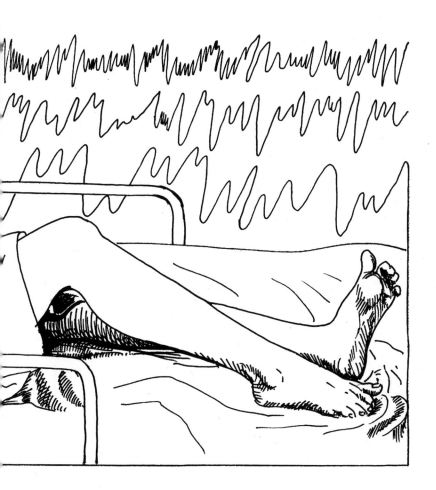

3:24   Even my neurologist, my new good neurologist,
        had kept the correlations to herself.

        And there was more
        that she had to know but hadn't mentioned.

        The amygdalae,
        the almond shaped hip pockets
        of fight or flight responses
        get overplayed, both during trauma
        and afterwards, with PTSD.
        Hypervigilance is physical.
        The whole limbic system
        is implicated.

        Even the hippocampus,
        that seahorse of memory,
        can be damaged.

        And stress hormones run rampant.
        And stress hormones run rampant.
        And stress hormones run rampant.

        I wondered what else I hadn't been told.

3:25   I found it when I googled PTSD and autoimmune disorders.

It was there, in the research, a correlation between trauma and disease.

Thank the VA.
Vets from Nam with PTSD are known to be more likely
to develop autoimmune disorders
than vets who just suffered the ordinary effects of war.

So my numb legs
the reason I threatened to hold up the MRI clinic
are linked, statistically at least, to having been pinned,
to having been molested, to having been traumatized
and retraumatized.

3:26   It was enough.

My corpus callosum.
My brainwaves.
My disease.
My fricking life.

It was all
I could take.

I turned the computer off
and went to bed.

I had no intention
of ever getting up again.

3:27   I woke up
vindicated.

I was not crazy.
I was never crazy.
I was simply not the predator.

Everything made sense.

From leaving my body
to burning my arm
everything made
perfectly horrible sense.

It was a first:
comprehension.

It was a relief:
clarity.

It was merited:
grief.

And it was not all there is
to the story.

Trauma is only a skeleton
I've finally dug from the closet

of my flesh. Life though,
my fricking life, is something else.

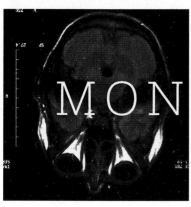

MONEYSHOT

The hymen in my head broke.

Picture a little mucous membrane in my thinking that separated my brain from my body. "As if my body lives here (point to the ground) but I live there (point to the sky)." That's how I described dissociation when I was in third grade. (I was living in England, hallucinating music daily, and happily enamored of my middle-name-sake Anne Boleyn and the fact that she'd had her head chopped off by Henry the 8th.) I clearly remember theorizing about the two realities I lived in because when I hit my second year of calculus in high school and started working with multiple dimensions, I experienced mathematical déjà vus back to grade school. Contemplating dissociation kept me intrigued enough to finish calculus despite the teacher's failed attempts to make me care about washers in the space shuttle.

I was split early and I stayed split for almost three decades.

One overdose, however, reminded me that my brain was still housed (unfortunately) in my body. In the middle of an art class, a couple hours after I'd popped the pills, the top of my skull went numb, along with my lips and an arm. I had to slur something akin to, "Hey Prof, I think I might have taken fifteen too many appetite suppressants before your class. Have you got a phone?"

I ended up at the ER.

After four hours hooked to an IV, I realized there was at least a one-way stomach-to-skull connection and that I still wanted to use my body, or at least not hurt my brain. Five weeks in the mental hospital reinforced that epiphany, and with one totally arbitrary exception, I never intentionally hurt my brain's vehicle again.

I stayed, however, out of body.

Then with the MS, my brain took a go at my dissociation.

Pow.

I was completely walloped. Having lesions in your brain that knock out your legs is terrifying. And weirdly unifying. I could almost see my body and head as one entity collaborating, however poorly, on everything from devastation to pleasure.

To then find out that all the traumas other people inflicted on my flesh might possibly have impacted more than just my thinking and behavior, that predators might have hurt my actual brain and health, that essentially nothing was sacred, was harrowing.

Frankly, the past penetrated the present.

Rip.

And yet, I'm not entirely devastated.

Passing out whenever people get too close is only convenient in theory. Ducking whenever anyone raises his or her voice is socially awkward. Not dating for a five-year stretch after experiencing attempted murder is less than satisfying, and blocking memories only leads to burbling flashbacks. Fight, flight, or freeze: I've done all of it, lived like an animal, adrenaline's puppet. And that sucks.

All I know is that now things are different.

My body owns everything.

As if I'm finally integrating the yuck.

Or beginning to.

I have to pace myself.

*

I was in the middle of running a 4x4 relay, coming in for the handoff, when I heard a voice from high in the stadium bleachers yell, "Go Wench Go!"

It was my father.

I had no doubt; not only was it unmistakably his voice but the very diction was the epitome of his brain. I wanted to keep running but I went ahead and passed the baton to my teammate, stumbled off the track onto the green and bent double, hugging my knees. That's the kind of thing you get to do when you're out of breath, the kind of thing you *have* to do when your father has just wenchified you in public and you want to pretend that you couldn't pick out that one genetically linked voice from the more generalized cheering and blur of adrenaline. I looked at my knees for the full minute it took my teammate to round the track, hoping no one would notice if I kept my head down.

Recently, a couple decades after that weird cheer, it became important to me to know if anyone, or rather someone in particular, had noticed: my mother. I called her, "Hi Mom," cutting straight to the chase, "Do you remember Dad yelling 'Go Wench Go' at a track meet?"

She wasn't thrown off at all.

"Oh yeah, I heard him."

And with that we laughed, me out of sheer relief that there was a witness to anything from my childhood, and her because, well, what else was there to do?

A father had used the word *wench* on his daughter in 1985.

Now I want to call up the neurologist who told me I'd have trouble with memory and say, "Guess what I remember."

After the neurologist told me that a smaller corpus callosum would cause me to have trouble with memory, I went into one of the biggest tizzies I've ever been in. My corpus callosum was responsible for leaving the oven on for twenty-four hours (with a tuna casserole inside), for misplaced keys, for forgetting a woman's name at a book signing, and for the word, oh god, the word on the tip of my tongue.

I am a writer. Was my vocabulary going to be reduced to the average diction of a karaoke machine? And what was I going to write if I couldn't remember that I saw a Gila monster in my driveway in the morning? And how was I going to live if I couldn't remember whom I could trust and whom I couldn't?

I panicked.

I started doing crosswords every morning. I started doing brain exercises out of books. I started corresponding with, and following instructions from, some scientist (or perhaps quack) in India that I'd met on the internet. (He had me using an egg timer and alternately reading scientific writing and fiction in ever shortening chunks of time.)

The neurological feeding frenzy has calmed as I've realized I'm still pretty functional, that most of my memory problems date back to childhood or specific traumas, and that's to be expected from sexual abuse. Most of my other forgetfulness is just the everyday kind that happens when you get distracted. I'm learning to cut myself some slack—without giving up.

What's surprising is this thing I feel akin to acceptance.

I want it—memory—and all that memory means, even the bad stuff.

Repression is busted.

I'm bigger than the fantasy of a good life.

I'm even bigger than my "mood-congruent" depression-induced fantasy of hell.

I'm all of it.

I want to be.

So give me the good, the bad, and the mediocre.

Who am I if I can't remember what it felt like to drive my knee into the sky, arch my back, fling my legs forward, and land on my butt seventeen feet and four inches from where I took off? A jump that won State my junior year in high school. Who am I if I can't remember being chased by my belt-wielding Viet Nam vet father into the bathroom where I cowered fully clothed in the tub? Who am I if I can't remember pouting in front of a field of daffodils?

*

My childhood memories remain fragmented. I see displaced genitals. I see a yellow and brown striped shirt with a seventies collar flapping in my face. I remember a hand inside me but I cannot see whose hand it is.

Amnesia makes you paranoid.

I have scoured my memories of childhood, family photos, old writings, everything I could find or recall, just trying to figure out who hurt me.

There were three main predators; it could have been any or all.

Once in a dream, I saw my father's face on a "WANTED" poster. A few times in my dreams I've been threatened by the military to keep my mouth shut. In hundreds of dreams, I've appeared as Raggedy Ann, the doll I had since birth. In those dreams I can't move or speak because I'm made of fabric and someone has their hand inserted up between my legs, as if—despite my conscious perception—I were a dumb puppet pulled from the toy box. In too many dreams, I can't run because my pants are pulled halfway down, limiting the movement of my thighs. When that happens, I resort to jumping, or a hobbled hopping.

Despite having body memories and flashbacks, I'll probably never know the full extent of what happened to me. Maybe there's not enough space on my corpus callosum for the information to traverse. Perhaps the black hole caused by multiple sclerosis burned parts out. Perhaps I'm not ready to remember more.

Or maybe, I'm just not ready to talk about all of it.

Even when I go through the tick lists of symptoms that survivors of early sexual violence experience, I mentally check off more than I am willing to count or put on paper.

I know enough: I know it happened.

At this point, I have to go on, figure out what to do now.

It should be easy.

It should be instinctual.

When I was little, I would cry on my rag doll's hand; Raggedy Ann would wipe my tears. And then later after I was done crying, I'd suck the salt back out of cloth and stuffing.

*

I called my mom back the day after I got the "wench" verification. Another question was pressing.

"So, what did you do? Did you say anything to him? Did you do anything?"

She laughed, as if it were still the prior day's conversation.

"What can you do?"

"So you didn't say anything?"

"No."

I have to admit, I got really upset about that, as if she'd somehow condoned my father's behavior.

As if she were complicit.

Then I remembered, I ran varsity track for four years and I only remember my father at one meet. Perhaps that's what my mom did for me, not drag him to another.

*

"What are you going to do?" is a good question when it's not in the context of an alcoholic father's behavior. It's a good question for me now. How am I going to react to all the statistics? My own doctors are bickering, even about the simplest information. The Centers for Disease Control [CDC] acknowledges that PTSD is actually a risk factor for violence. Revictimization rates are undeniably higher for survivors of early sexual abuse. Although my doctors can't argue with that fact, they harbor different opinions as to why. Lack of coping strategies? Maladaptive efforts at self-medicating? Vulnerability due directly to symptoms of PTSD, like dissociation? Something more esoteric, something energy-based or happening below the level of consciousness, that lets predators spot you in a crowd? (Most of the trauma victims I've met also feel, as I do, as if we have a sign on our foreheads beckoning more violence towards us.)

Consequently, my doctors certainly can't agree on the significance of what Harvard psychiatrist Martin Teicher found: a smaller corpus callosum (smaller in the middle, which is where mine is thin) in survivors of early sexual abuse. And abuse is not the only potential cause of this diminishment; I personally might be tempted to think my corpus callosum is simply smaller due to MS (which can happen) if it weren't for the fact that I already had symptoms of a smaller corpus callosum (like severe dissociation and memory gaps) in early childhood. Even the electrical changes and the temporal lobe imbalance noted on my EEG can be correlated with abuse or predisposed by a smaller corpus callosum. It's confusing.

*

I want hard proof that what happened took both an emotional and physical toll, but no certain cause and effect is 100% certain.

All we have as evidence are "correlations."

Why is that all there is? That's all there is because you can't ethically take a random sampling of the population and subject them to sexual abuse and trauma and see what happens. You can't make good hard science out of violence.

As close as a random sampling gets (as far as I'm concerned) is the military. Large groups of people who were "fit" before wars end up with PTSD afterwards. The Veterans Administration then tracks their health. To me, that looks like a pretty big (and costly) experiment. The percentage for vets with an autoimmune disorder is undeniably higher for vets who have PTSD. Add a secondary diagnosis of another mental health disorder and the numbers jump again. Now, new evidence is coming to light that shows a greater risk of coronary problems in vets with PTSD. The correlations are there. It's *the whys* that are little understood. Perhaps some biological change caused by PTSD leads to increased risk. Or, perhaps some *behavioral* change caused by PTSD has biological ramifications. Nobody knows. Yet.

I read and read and read.

*

And I know a little bit and consequently believe a few things. Because early sexual abuse can change the brain's structure, as well as disrupt the chemical and electrical balance, I believe that's what happened to me. Those changes, when partnered with other things like lack of healthy coping strategies, mean that victims of early sexual abuse are likely prey for later victimization—and so I believe that for a wide range of reasons, my childhood "slated me" for more abuse in adulthood. And as trauma's aftermath of PTSD is correlated to all kinds of negative health outcomes, including the possibility of autoimmune disorders, and because I've lived with the inordinately high stress of active PTSD for decades, I believe that PTSD has definitely impacted my health negatively. Although I believe multiple sclerosis has multiple triggers, I believe that, at least for me, trauma is one of the things that helped set disease into motion.

Ultimately, I'd argue that what was done to me before the age of two (as my first memory is recognizably that of a child between 18 and 24 months) set into motion the machinery of escalating victimization and deteriorating health.

*

Confronted with all the information and with how I feel about it, my cognitive therapist shakes his head *no* (or he used to, now he listens and asks questions) while my PTSD counselor and psychiatrist nod *yes*.

So far no one can convince me that trauma doesn't take a huge emotional and physical toll. Even the World Health Organization came out with a study showing that women who'd been victims of domestic violence suffered "generally poorer health" later in life than women who hadn't had to survive violence. Try to tell me trauma doesn't matter. The evidence is overwhelming and indicting.

I know.

I'm living it.

*

Now what? I have to go on. I have to develop an identity that is capable of both acknowledging what happened and transcending it. Everybody has to do this, one way or another. My father, when I used to go to restaurants with him in my twenties, would immediately announce to the waitress, even before the drink orders:

"I'm not an old letch; she's my daughter."

That was his version of a truth.

As for mine? I'm a helluva lot more than the daughter of an old letch.

I'm more than anything that's happened to me.

I'm even more than my disease.

I'm everything.

Body and brain.

The head of the Nile is in three degrees south latitude, where in the year 1858, I discovered the head of the Victoria N'yanza to be. . . . I spent the day watching the fish flying at the falls, and felt as if I only wanted a wife and family, garden and yacht, rifle and rod, to make me happy here for life, so charming was the place. . . .

A boy, finding the king alone, walked up to him and threatened to kill him becasue he took the lives of men unjustly. When the youth attacked him, [the king] had in his hand the revolving pistol I had given him . . . and presented the muzzle to the boy, which, though it was unloaded, so frightened him that he ran away.

JOHN HANNING SPEKE
The Discovery of the Source of the Nile
1863

How to Live with It

a roller-coaster ride toward redemption

4:1   You'd think
this is where I get to put something
besides a shotgun in my hands.

A lily.
A lightbulb.
A river.
A photograph of Freud.
My own MRIs.
Anything but a Brazilian 12-gauge sawed off at both ends.

But a Brazilian 12-gauge sawed off at both ends
is what I picked up
when I threatened to hold up the MRI clinic.

And the shotgun, as if organic, as if malleable,
—as if still in my hands—
winds around my self concept.

Self-preservation is instinct.
Sometimes it kicks in.
Sometimes it kicks in the door to self-knowledge.

So I am not so gentle
as I'd thought.

So I am not so non-
violent.

So I was not the predator
but I speak the language.

Violence is learned
and I've been schooled.

This is not the epiphany
I wanted.

I wanted the big one,
the one that wakes
you up,
that resurrects you
from memory,
the one that lets you
live as if nothing
ever happened.

Instead I got a gun.

4:2   You want to know where I got the shotgun?

I got the shotgun from a friend.
It landed in his possession via an arc over a fence.
Someone tossed it, middle of the night.
Someone tossed it in the middle of the night before a morning
when my friend's kids would wake, start playing, and find it.

Score one for something—this time the gun was already fired
and luckily not reloaded.

4:3   Funny what sticks out in my mind
after everything. (The shotgun.)
It's not so much what was done to me,
as how I responded. (The shotgun.)

Violence is learned and I've been schooled.

And if I don't want to repeat the crimes,
this is nonetheless where I go ahead
and shove my knee into this culture's groin.
This is where I don't apologize.

(Shotgun shotgun shotgun.)

I'm not sorry.

(Shotgun shotgun shotgun.)

I can still breathe and walk so I won't grovel,
I'm no martyr,
no turn-the-other-cheek girl,
no victim . . .
                anymore.

This is where I open my mouth
and say publicly:

       I did what I had to do.

This is where I open my mouth
and say publicly:

       Don't fuck with me.

4:4 Because blood, breath, and semen,
I don't want to be vulnerable anymore.

Ever.

For over a decade I've been living outside city limits
because the predators per capita may be the same
but the acreage between them is not.

Some days I don't even want to shake a hand
without taking a DNA sample.

Once I accepted a grilled cheese sandwich from a stranger.
I thought it was a gesture of kindness.
Then, he took me and raped me.
I have never eaten a grilled cheese sandwich since.

Of course, I don't eat mandarin oranges anymore either.

Nothing is innocuous
when you're dealing with humans.

4:5   What happened makes me want to vomit.
        This is how it hits me.
        What didn't kill me didn't make my stomach stronger.

        Understand: I am not a toll-free number with all the right
        answers about violence.

        I am just a woman who's been through some shit.

        A friend asks,

"How do you
live with it?"

4:6   What am I supposed to do?

Die?

I nearly did,
over and over,
and it wasn't particularly satisfying
so I can think of better responses
although I did have one
near-death experience
at seventeen that was at least intriguing.
I floated out of my body, saw the bright lights,
the whole warm fuzzy deal, but even then I knew
       because I had to make a conscious decision to come back
that I wanted to be here.

4:7   So I say, simply, "I live just like you do.
I have an autonomic nervous system.
Without even having to think about it,
my heart beats and blood courses.
I inhale and I exhale. Waste gets processed. . . ."

I like that so I repeat it,

"Waste gets processed. The body does
what the body does to sustain basic human life.
Et cetera. Et cetera.
I live with it by not being dead yet."

4:8   In other words I live—
ordinary phenomenon.

Sleep and dream.
Wake and work.

There are groceries and dishes.
Telephone calls and appointments.
Friends to see.

Books to read.
Books to write.
Books that make me forget to water the houseplants.
Houseplants that wilt and make me put down the books long enough
to get a pitcher of water and pour it.

I watch the stars.
I cross the Rubicon.
I eat apricots and let my lover hold me.
I let my cat, and only my cat, walk all over me.

I remember time.
Violence is the least of my life.

Minutes to hours anyway,
it's not the half of it.

4:9   Violence does funny things to the brain.
I'm breathing
but sometimes in the middle of the night
that doesn't matter.
God says, "How do you live with it?"
And I say, "I don't."

For two years after my lover tried to kill me, I hardly left the house.
What do you call that? Coffin? Sarcophagus? Adobe urn?

Breathing isn't always living.

    Memory is a parasite.
    Memory is a machete, a car accident, a fainting couch.
    Memory is molecular.

Sometimes I curl up fetal with flashbacks.
Sometimes I gag, I shake, I vomit.
Sometimes I call the toll-free number that has all the right answers to
violence.
Sometimes I don't.
Sometimes I die.

I have spent one thousand nights on that examining table with my
feet in stirrups
and I ask you,

How much blood must I lose before I quit saying I'm fine?

4:10   I'm not fine.
The boxer tried to take my legs off.
A lover cursed at me for ten minutes after sex.
A doctor said prude.

A man in a passing car threw rocks
as I tried to walk down the street
with another woman.

My brain is damaged.
My body scarred.
Disease has set in.

And I have not yet had the big epiphany,
the one that wakes you,
the one that resurrects you from memory,
the one that lets you live as if nothing ever happened.

Truth: I will never get to live as if nothing ever happened.
Truth: I don't want to. . . .

           Anymore.

4:11   Because I've already tried taking the proverbial shower
and I can tell you, it doesn't work.

Here's why: there is not enough water in the world.

A week, a month, a year later, you're gonna freak out
that you might have contracted something.

And a decade after that, you're gonna scour your body
wishing you could find just one foreign pubic hair
because survival is not enough, the violence has to stop
and this is when you wish you had proof of something.

4:12   So yes, I wish I'd pressed charges.
I wish I'd reported the malpractice.
I wish I'd done anything
to stop any of the people who hurt me
from hurting one more woman,
so I am doing what I can do now:

I am sicking my skinny corpus callosum on the world.

Because what's horrific is not what happened to me,
it's that I'm not alone.
            I am no fluke.
            No freak.
            I am not even rare.
            And it wasn't my fault.
            I didn't ask for it.
            I wasn't wearing the wrong clothes.
            I didn't deserve it.
            I am not even "unlucky."
And I was not in the wrong place at the wrong time:

This is the wrong culture at the wrong time.

4:13 So read the statistics. Or don't.
Put a face on the numbers. Or don't.
Wonder if teeth are missing. Or don't.
Take your morning shower and remember what it can mean. Or don't.

If this is the wrong culture at the wrong time,
it's also nothing new.
Violence is an old story. A cross-cultural story.

Entrenched.
Ingrained.
Systemic.

And learned.

Insurmountable?

4:14   What's insurmountable?

I climbed to the top of the Zugspitz when I was a child.
I pushed a man who was choking me off my body with a knee.
I got my MRI.

And I live with it.

4:15   If there is not enough water in the Thames,
If there is not enough water in the Nile,
If there is not enough water in the Rio Grande during the monsoons,
If there is not enough water in the world
to undo what has happened,

DID I TELL YOU

There is enough water in one individual body
for liberation.

Here is the epiphany:
I have to make my own catharsis.

I LOVE

House of cards.
Cardboard box.
Card table with a sheet over it.
Frame and stucco with a blue tin roof.
Flesh.

I've fallen for the idea I'm not helpless.
I've fallen for the idea I can do something.
I've fallen for the idea I can thrive.

LIFE!?

131

4:16   Because I want to.
        Because I can.

        If trauma stunts the development of the brain,
        If violence releases a cascade of stress hormones the body rides like
        whitewater rapids,
        If PTSD opens the door to disease,

        Who is tabulating the ramifications of one good conversation?

                                    or a book,
                                    a caress,
                                    a walk with dogs,
                                    yoga on a mat,
                                    or a bad joke you can't resist making?

        Tally this:
        Comparing Chinese Pictograms and Japanese Kanji at the truck stop.

        Tally this:
        Listening to Monk and pining for your own Nellie at dusk.

        Tally this:
        Seeing a toad in the middle of the high desert at midnight after the monsoons.

        Tally this:
        Gambling with marbles for marbles on the gutter grate in grade school
        and winning.

        Tally this:
        Getting your MRI and knowing you didn't imagine it.

        Tally this:
        Calling the crap crap.

4:17   I am lucid.
I am sane.
I am speaking.
I am holding this culture accountable.
Because I have to.
Because I want to.

Because women matter
and I know
I am not alone.

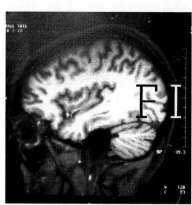

FISHBONE

I was born March 16, 1970 and became shy on August 1, 1970. My mother marked it on her calendar. She gave the calendar to me a few years back because she thought I might like the images—medieval illuminations of the Revelation of St. John. Instead I checked out all her notations. In the little box under that Saturday in August, it reads simply, "Lisa became shy today."

Seven days later it reads, "Lisa broke a plate from Mom's table."

*

Apparently, as a toddler I hid behind my mother's leg whenever we encountered another person. That story sticks with me. But it's more than a story. It's how I am sometimes.

*

When I tried out for the role of Lady Macbeth in our fifth grade Shakespeare Club, none of the students or teachers had ever heard me raise my voice. I remember how it felt, to break the silence wide open with that soliloquy and bash babies' brains out all around the portable classroom.

I got the part.

*

The first time I was considered a threat to society was when I was still a military brat. I was in Germany and I'd taped open the lock on a door. My intent was to let us get back into the classroom after recess. It was cold and our teacher, probably a lush, was always late to return.

They called the MP's.

Apparently they thought the tape was an

attempt to aid terrorists. They came with guns to the classroom and threatened us with jail.

I never told anyone that it was me and they never figured it out.

*

Until recently, the word that came to mind when I thought of myself was *mousification*. At twenty, after a year of puffed sleeves and wrap-around skirts, I quit waitressing. I didn't think I could afford to be polite any longer. It felt dangerous. I'd said, "No thank you," to a man who'd pulled his car up beside me and asked me to get in. I'd said "No thank you" even after I saw him jacking off.

*

A not particularly close friend brought me a strawberry at a party. I was wall-flowered, so far removed from the goings on that I was startled by the gesture of kindness. This happens over and over.

*

Another friend thinks the story of threatening to hold up the MRI clinic is anticlimactic simply because I left the shotgun at home. I don't agree. Language, even spoken quietly, is powerful.

And now, the shotgun is an artifact of a bigger story.

*

My best friend of the past decade doesn't think I'm shy or good. He thinks I was just told I had to be quiet and behave when I was little.

Now he thinks I'm wiley.

It's true.

At least at thirty-three, I did exactly what was necessary. No more, no less. There were a number of possible scenarios I could have chosen, but when the ER dismissed me, I went to the mental hospital to make my threat.

My mom says, repeatedly, "I'm so glad you knew what to do because I didn't."

*

Perhaps the ER doctors didn't intend to paralyze me, but by refusing to treat me, by dismissing me as crazy, there was a chance I'd lose my legs.

Intent matters to me. As does the end result.

I did what I had to do.

It worked.

And it made the local alternative newspaper.

I was lucky. The reporter's father had been struck by lightning while riding a bicycle and that dictated how the story was focused. He'd perked up when he learned that the flare coincided with a

lightning strike in the sky and that I'd mistaken a neurological problem for exposure to external electrical current.

Moreover, he astutely picked up on my one telling sentence in an eight thousand word chapbook about MS and asked me about the threat.

I spoke.

I spoke out of guilt.

I spoke out of a desire for public absolution.

It *almost* worked. He didn't sensationalize my bad behavior until halfway through the article. I was relieved. Most people would never read that far.

It was in the Arts Section.

Every year I make the same New Year's resolution, to speak out the same way I do in dreams, to be forthright and assertive. I'm getting closer.

I got invited to show art and read poetry at a gathering of neurologists. They were going to celebrate the new brain research facility with a keynote speaker on the latest news in multiple sclerosis. I was going to represent people living with MS.

I sat down for my interview with a bit of trepidation. I didn't know how they'd found out about me. I didn't know if they knew my story.

The neurologist began asking me about my MS. I told her that I'd gone undiagnosed for almost a decade, that instead I'd been given mental health labels.

She said, "Oh, you're one of those."

As our talk and the tour of the facility progressed, she gradually whittled down my role to sitting at a table and "talking with the wives."

Deep inside my brain there is a *Futility Index*. I can almost see a red dial on the gauge rising. When it goes off, sometimes I still say nothing, defer quietly or nod, but now I remember that I'm angry.

And that's when I know, it's not over.

My bad behavior.

My fight.

Illustrations

Kris Mills

Acknowledgements

I owe a debt of gratitude to many people for helping me along the journey for this book, the first of whom are my doctors—two neurologists, one psychiatrist, one trauma counselor, and a cognitive behavioral therapist—all who helped me survive 2003 and begin to process the dual onslaught of physical change and ferocious knowledge.

Friends and colleagues have as thoroughly aided the actual writing process as doctors did my medical progress. The poems for this book were written in 2005, two years after I threatened to hold up the MRI clinic. After over a year of physical therapy during which I wrote *Mortar & Pestle* in response to my diagnosis, I was finally well enough to begin contemplating *how* I got my diagnosis. When I began, the eighty-nine poems of this book poured out and didn't let up until they were finished. During that time, Mitch Rayes, as he often is, was the first reader and supporter of my work.

Upon completion, I took the text to Virginia Hampton of Out ch'Yonda (a performance space in Albuquerque, New Mexico) and asked if she would direct a one-woman-show of the poems. She agreed. One of the first and most significant questions she asked me was, "Where is this set?" Without hesitating, I answered, "The Garden of Eternal Justice." That response led us to ask Kris Mills and Liz Hunt to create the busts of Freud, Sanger, Teicher, and Speke to be set upon pedestals alongside a fountain. During each act, I opened cans of mandarin oranges and poured them into the fountain. Between acts, we had black-n-white-n-orange film interludes provided by Bryan Konefsky. Stefanie Willis did the lighting and technical work and Mitch Rayes composed music for show. We premiered *Caput Nili* in March of 2006.

Melody Sumner Carnahan and Michael Sumner of Burning Books saw the show the first weekend and had the vision to turn *Caput Nili* into a book. Before the run was over, I had an invitation to publish the work. In contemplating a book, I decided that I wanted to add essays, four of which I went on to write in Joy Harjo's Creative Nonfiction Workshop my first semester in graduate school at the University of New Mexico in the fall of 2006. The fifth essay stymied me for another year, but thanks to the support and inspiration of many students and colleagues and professors, including Greg Martin, Laura Matter, Molly Beer, and Christina Yovovich, I eventually completed the text. Burning Books also encouraged incorporating art, and I elected to work with illustrations by Kris Mills, one of my longtime collaborators. After all the pieces came together, Melody Sumner Carnahan and Michael Sumner teased out a beautiful prototype, which won two awards for design from the New Mexico Book Association in 2010.

And now, John Crawford of West End Press is releasing the first trade edition. I thank him profoundly, thank Burning Books, thank everyone listed here, and thank you, the reader. This has been quite the journey already, and it's just getting started.

Kris Mills received her B.A. in Fine Art from the University of California at Davis and her M.F.A. from the University of New Mexico. She has won numerous awards at venues including the *Invitational Du Voyager Symposium Snow Sculpture Competition* (Canada), "Fuzzy Logic" in *Southern Exposure* (San Francisco), and the Friends of Art Award and People's Choice Award for the *Roads to Chaos* exhibition (Albuquerque). She has received scholarships, fellowships, and residencies throughout the country and often serves as a guest lecturer. Her solo and group art and photography exhibitions have appeared regionally, nationally, and internationally, at such diverse locations as the Niagara Arts Center, the University of Alabama Gallery of Photography, and the Musee de L'Elysee. "The Nerve," an exhibition in collaboration with Lisa Gill, was named one of the top ten arts events of Albuquerque in 2005 by the *Weekly Alibi*. For over fifteen years, Mills has worked for the renowned artist Joel-Peter Witkin, building and painting sets, backdrops, and props for his photographs, which exhibit internationally.

Lisa Gill is the recipient of a National Endowment for the Arts Fellowship in Poetry, a Gratitude Award from New Mexico Literary Arts, and an Achievement Award from the University of New Mexico, where she received an M.F.A. with distinction in 2010. She has published four previous books of poetry, including *Red as a Lotus: Letters to a Dead Trappist, Mortar & Pestle, Dark Enough,* and *The Relenting: A Play of Sorts.* The NEA selected one of her poems to represent Literature Fellowships in their Annual Report to the President of the United States for 2007 and both her poetry and prose have been widely published and anthologized. She has performed her work across the U.S., from Beyond Baroque in Los Angeles to New York's Bowery Poetry Club, also reading at the Thomas McGrath Visiting Writer's Series in Minnesota, the Seattle Poetry Festival, and the Taos Poetry Circus in New Mexico. A long-term New Mexico resident, she now lives in Albuquerque, where she has participated in events for the Church of Beethoven, 516 ARTS, the Civil Rights Symposium, and the Women Braving Violence Conference. Gill frequently collaborates with artists, musicians, and filmmakers.